W9-CJD-538

BLACK EXPLORERS

A M E R I C A N
P R O F I L E S

BLACK EXPLORERS

■

Catherine Reef

Facts On File, Inc.

AN INFOBASE HOLDINGS COMPANY

Black Explorers

Copyright © 1996 by Catherine Reef

Facts On File, Inc.
11 Penn Plaza
New York NY 10001

Library of Congress Cataloging-in-Publication Data

Reef, Catherine.
   Black explorers / Catherine Reef.
      p. cm. — (American profiles)
   Includes bibliographical references and index.
   Contents: Esteban — Jean-Baptiste Pointe du Sable — James
Beckwourth — Charles Young — Matthew Henson — Albert Jose Jones —
   Guion S. Bluford — Mae C. Jemison.
   Summary: Profiles eight black explorers, ranging from pioneers of
the 1700s to people working today.
   ISBN 0-8160-3315-3 (alk. paper)
   1. Afro-American explorers—Biography—Juvenile literature.
[1. Explorers. 2. Afro-Americans—Biography.] I. Title.
II. Series: American profiles (Facts On File, Inc.)
G225.R44 1996
920'.009296073—dc20
[B]   95-51552

Cover design by Matt Galemmo

Illustrations by Jeremy Eagle, Patricia Meschino, and Dale Williams

Printed in the United States of America

MP FOF 10 9 8 7 6 5 4 3 2 1

This book is printed on acid-free paper.

Contents

Introduction

Even in the days when the Negro had little or no opportunity to show his ability as a leader, he proved himself at least a splendid follower, and there are few great adventures in which the American white man has engaged where he has not been accompanied by a colored man.

*T*hose words, written by the black educator Booker T. Washington, were published in 1912. Washington included them in his introduction to the autobiography of Matthew Henson, African-American explorer and codiscoverer of the North Pole. Henson's knowledge of Arctic survival skills and expertise as a dog-sled driver were essential to his expedition's success. And it was Henson, and not his white fellow explorer, Robert Peary, who first stood at the pole in 1909. Yet for many years, Peary alone was credited with discovering the North Pole. If Henson received recognition, it was for being Peary's black servant.

Booker T. Washington was correct in saying that people of African descent have played a part in most great exploratory ventures—though, like Henson, they often were more than merely followers. The curiosity and love of adventure that make for an explorer are present in individuals of every race and ethnic group.

Archaeological findings show that human beings were exploring their planet as early as 600 B.C. At that time, the Egyptian pharaoh Necho II dispatched a fleet of ships to circumnavigate Africa.

In the 15th and 16th centuries, when Europeans were exploring the New World, black men were often among their ships' crews, and at times held positions of responsibility. Some were free blacks who had been living in Europe. Others were slaves, the spoils of voyages to the African coast. It has been claimed, but not proved, that at least one crewman on Columbus's first voyage, Pedro Alonzo Niño of the ship *Niña*, was black. Scholars do know that 30 blacks were with Vasco Núñez de Balboa when he discovered the Pacific Ocean in 1513. People of African descent accompanied the Spaniard Hernán Cortés to Mexico in 1519, and were among the force commanded by Francisco Pizarro when he took over Peru in the 1530s.

After 1500, thousands of blacks crossed the Atlantic Ocean in Spanish ships. The Spaniards brought black slaves to New Spain, or Mexico, and set them to work mining gold and silver in Central and South America, on Caribbean islands, and in New Spain itself. According to one early historian, there were 10,000 blacks in the New World by 1528.

A slave named Estéban sailed to Florida with an expedition led by a Spanish nobleman, Pánfilo de Narváez, in 1527. Narváez's goal was conquest, so after his ships landed at Tampa Bay, his party quickly moved inland. The Spanish conquistadores in their heavy armor and brocades dropped from heat and disease in Florida's subtropical forests. Following Indian attacks and a hurricane, only four members of the expedition survived. One was Estéban.

Circumstances made Estéban, and not Narváez, an explorer. During the eight years he and his companions roamed the American Southwest, Estéban learned to survive in the wilderness and to communicate with the native tribes. He later guided the Spanish priest Father Marcos de Niza on a search for a legendary horde of treasure, the Seven Cities of Cibola. He led the priest's party into unexplored regions of present-day Arizona. Yet for years the Spaniard Francisco Vásquez de Coronado, and not Estéban, was credited with first exploring the Southwest.

Soon, more and more Europeans were venturing into the interior of North America. Catholic priests, such as the Frenchman Jacques Marquette, hoped to convert the Indians to Christianity. Fur traders, including Marquette's countryman Louis Jolliet, sought wealth from the continent's animal resources. In 1673, Marquette and Jolliet paddled their canoes along unknown waterways, becoming the first Europeans to follow the Mississippi River to the mouth of the Arkansas River. A black man made the journey with them.

Introduction

As settlers came to North America in growing numbers, blacks—both slave and free—continued to add to the knowledge of the continent. A township in Minnesota is named for the Bongas, a family of black trappers who explored the region in the 18th century.

Also during that century, a black trapper from Haiti named Jean-Baptiste Pointe du Sable boated up the Mississippi River. He came to a flat, fertile stretch of land alongside Lake Michigan that was called Eschikagou by the Native Americans. Recognizing the plain as an important link between the lake and tributaries of the Mississippi for pioneers moving west, Pointe du Sable established a trading post and settlement there. From that humble beginning, the City of Chicago grew. However, Pointe du Sable's contribution, like that of Estéban, was obscured for many years. Chicago's citizens credited a white trader, John Kinzie, with founding their city.

Throughout much of the period of exploration, England had been establishing colonies on the east coast of North America. Those colonies declared their independence in 1776. And almost as soon as their people achieved victory in the Revolutionary War, in 1781, they looked westward to expand their young nation. Under President Thomas Jefferson, the United States acquired an enormous tract of land in 1803. Known as the Louisiana Purchase, this largely unexplored region stretched from the Mississippi River to the Rocky Mountains. Its acquisition doubled the size of the United States.

Jefferson dispatched an exploratory expedition, led by Meriwether Lewis and William Clark, to traverse the newly acquired land and beyond, to report on the resources, terrain, and Native Americans they encountered. A slave named York was an invaluable member of the Lewis and Clark Expedition.

By 1860, the outline of the continental United States looked just as it does today. For 20 years, a steady stream of pioneers had already been moving west across the prairie and into Oregon and California. Colorful characters called mountain men roamed the western states and territories, trapping animals for fur and trading with the Native Americans. Having knowledge of the land and friendships with the Indians, the mountain men often guided pioneer wagon trains to their destinations.

One of the most flamboyant mountain men was James Beckwourth, an African American. Beckwourth was born a slave, but was granted his freedom in 1824. At various times a trader, prospector, innkeeper, explorer, and adopted member of the Crow tribe, he discovered a pass through the Sierra Nevada that eased the journey to California for many travelers.

Charles Young, too, was born into slavery. He gained his freedom while still a baby, when the Civil War ended in 1865. Yet, like all of the newly free members of his race, he soon learned that freedom did not mean equality in the United States of America. Determined to have a career as an army officer, Young endured snubbing and cruelty at the United States Military Academy. The leaders of the segregated army denied him opportunities to lead troops, instead giving him noncombat positions. Despite his disappointment, Young made the most of his assignments. As military attaché to Haiti and Liberia in the early 20th century, he explored and mapped unknown regions and gathered valuable information for the United States government.

As the century progressed, explorers entered new realms and harsher environments. Matthew Henson, Robert Peary, and others braved the storms and subzero temperatures of the polar regions. The invention of the Aqua-Lung in 1942 gave human beings the ability to move freely under water and led to greater exploration of marine environments. And African Americans have added to our knowledge of the seas. The marine scientist and college professor Albert José Jones, for example, has surveyed and mapped undersea regions and studied the animals that make the sea their home.

Today's explorers understand the need to protect the environment. For this reason, a large part of Jones's work now involves teaching both his students and foreign governments to preserve and restore fragile offshore ecosystems.

Introduction

Technology also has enabled men and women to travel in space. In 1961, the first American astronaut, Alan Shepard, flew to the edge of the atmosphere. Astronauts orbited Earth in the years that followed, and even walked on the Moon. Yet it was not until 1983 that an African American, Guion S. Bluford Jr., went into space. Mae C. Jemison became the first African-American woman to travel aboard a spacecraft in 1992.

Back in 1912, Booker T. Washington observed that doors had opened for his race since the days of slavery. Yet the changes he saw appear modest when compared to the gains of the middle decades of the 20th century. The protests of the civil rights years (1954–1965) brought about landmark Supreme Court decisions outlawing segregation in schools and on public transportation. Civil rights legislation guaranteed people of all races the right to vote and to be served in restaurants, hotels, and other places of business.

Segregation ended in the United States armed forces in 1948, and the military has led the rest of the nation in giving African Americans an equal chance to excel. Guy Bluford, whose years as an astronaut were the culmination of an Air Force career, had an experience very different from that of Charles Young. Bluford insists that he never encountered racial barriers in the Air Force. Many people, however, contend that the branches of the service still are not colorblind.

Today's African-American explorers—Jones, Bluford, Jemison, and others—know that their success can inspire young people to achieve. Like many Americans, they are concerned about the young blacks living in inner-city neighborhoods throughout the nation. Faced with racism and poverty, these boys and girls often feel unwanted by society. Many are tempted to drop out of school, use drugs, or join gangs.

Jones has spent countless hours instructing the youth of his hometown, Washington, D.C., in the two activities he most enjoys, scuba diving and tae kwon do. With the mastery of a skill, he has learned, come self-confidence and the desire to succeed. For this reason, he never counts people out. "All they need is opportunity and somebody who has confidence in them," he has said.

Bluford speaks to audiences of black youth, urging them to work hard and take advantage of opportunities that come their way. He tells African-American children, "I want you to be the future astronauts flying in space with me." He encourages them to excel, whether they want to be astronauts or to pursue other dreams. He says, "It's very important to set high goals for yourself and realize that if you work hard you will get them."

The African-American explorers of our time carry on a proud tradition of discovery. They are splendid leaders, rather than followers. For them, life is a continuing adventure.

Estéban
(c. 1500–c. 1539)

Ships from Spain and Portugal often docked at ports along the northwest coast of Africa in the 16th century. The Europeans captured cities and towns for their empires, and they took people into slavery. Portugal seized the ancient city of Azemmour, in present-day Morocco, in 1513. Not long afterward, a boy left the city on a Portuguese ship. He was taken to Spain and sold to a man named Andres Dorantes, who called the boy Estéban.

Sailing ships were also making voyages across the Atlantic Ocean to lands that had been unheard of in Europe just a few decades earlier. Now, explorers went to the New World to claim territory for the king of Spain. They brought back gold, stories of strange peoples, and legends of vast wealth in unexplored inland regions.

In June 1527, five ships set sail from Spain, commanded by a nobleman, Pánfilo de Narváez. King Charles I had commissioned Narváez to explore and conquer unknown lands from Florida to the Rio Grande, and to form settlements along the way. Andres Dorantes and his slave Estéban were among the men who accompanied Narváez.

Estéban was beginning the adventure that would earn him a place in the history of exploration. He would survive the Indian attacks, storms, diseases, hunger, and thirst that wiped out most members of the Narváez expedition. He would spend eight years crossing the continent of North America, almost from sea to sea, traveling over mountains, deserts, and rivers that no one but Indians had ever seen. In 1539, he would lead the way for a Spanish expedition into land that is now part of the American Southwest.

———

After three months of sailing, Narváez's ships reached the island of Hispaniola, where Spain had established its first colony in the Americas. They then pushed on to Santiago, Cuba. The ships took on horses and supplies at each port and delivered cargoes of slaves.

Because Estéban had come to serve his master, he stayed with the expedition. He was one of the 400 men aboard the five ships when Florida's west coast came into view, on April 12, 1528. As the explorers entered Tampa Bay and neared the shore, they saw the huts of an Indian village in the distance.

The expedition's treasurer, Álvar Núñez Cabeza de Vaca, later wrote an account of his experiences in the New World. He noted that "On Good Friday, Governor Narváez landed with as many men as his little boats would hold. And when we arrived at the huts we had seen, we found them abandoned. The Indians had fled that night in their canoes." Wasting no time, Narváez claimed the deserted village for Spain. He named the region La Bahia de la Cruz, meaning Bay of the Cross.

Some of the Indians, who were members of the Timucuan tribe, wandered back the next day. The Spaniards used gestures to ask them where food and riches could be found. The Timucuan told of a place to the north called Apalachen where the people were wealthy.

Narváez and 300 of his men set out for Apalachen on May 2, with four Timucuan as guides. The rest of the Spanish party returned to the ships. While one ship sailed back to Cuba for food, the other four moved up the coast. Narváez and his followers planned to meet up with them after conquering Apalachen.

A sketch of the Timucuan chief Saturiova by Jacques Le Moyne de Morques, the first European artist in North America. The Timucuan covered their bodies with tattoos commemorating battles and hunts.
(Peabody Museum, Harvard University. Photo by Hillel Burger)

Estéban and Dorantes went with Narváez on the long, tough march. Half of the 80 horses died of illness and starvation on the way. The men were hungry, too. Each had only two pounds of sea biscuit and a half pound of bacon to keep him going.

They helped themselves to corn growing beside Indian villages they passed, and they foraged for berries. After six weeks of marching, they reached the territory of the Apalachee people. Their guides pointed out the largest village, Apalachen.

The Spaniards found only women and children living there. The men apparently had fled. The explorers searched the houses for gold, but they found none. They discovered plenty of dried corn, though, and they forced the women to grind it for mush.

All at once, the Apalachee men emerged from hiding places around the village to attack the invaders with bows and arrows. The Indian warriors ran off when all their arrows had been used, but they returned the next day with more arrows and 200 men from another village. The Indians attacked again and again, wounding Spaniards, slaves, and horses. "The good armor we wore was no help," wrote Cabeza de Vaca. The Apalachee arrows went right through it. Estéban and the other slaves wore no armor at all.

The Spaniards fought back with their crossbows as well as they could, but they were losing many men. Those still alive decided to sneak away, return to the shore, and await rescue by their ships. The escape route took them through thick forests where Indians shot at them from behind trees, and swamps where mosquitoes passed on malaria.

At last, the men reached a cove. They waited for days but saw no sign of their ships. They finally decided to build boats of their own. They melted down their crossbows and arrows and pounded the molten metal into tools for felling trees and shaping timbers. To survive, they ate corn and beans that they stole from Indians' fields, and they butchered their horses for meat.

The crews of the ships, meanwhile, searched the Florida coast, but they never spotted Narváez and the others. A year later, they sailed to Cuba and reported the expedition lost.

The abandoned men built five barges, each 30 feet long, and each to carry nearly 50 men. When the barges were launched and everyone squeezed aboard, only 6 inches of each boat showed above the water, and the crews could barely move! The vessels traveled westward toward Mexico, known then as New Spain, where there were several Spanish settlements. But they stayed near the coastline, so that Estéban and the other slaves could wade ashore to look for food and drinking water. Some of the men grew so thirsty that they drank the salty sea water, and five died as a result.

Hunger and thirst were not the only hazards now. In November 1528, the five crowded barges ran into a severe storm on the Gulf of Mexico that might have been a hurricane. The heavy winds and rough waves carried the boats away from land and out of sight of one another.

Estéban, Dorantes, and their entire crew survived the storm. The waves carried their battered barge to a narrow, sandy island off the coast of what is now Texas. They called the island Malhado, meaning "ill fate." For much of the year, Malhado was the home of two groups of Indians, the Capoque and the Han. These were nomadic people who lived in houses fashioned from mats of woven rushes. From February through April, they lived on the mainland, where they harvested oysters and foraged for berries.

The native people took in the Spaniards and their slaves, and fed them fish and root vegetables. Estéban and his companions soon learned that Cabeza de Vaca's barge had beached elsewhere on the island and that he and some of his crew had survived. The other three barges, including the one that carried Narváez, were never heard from again.

Some of the Spaniards and Indians came down with dysentery, an illness that causes severe diarrhea. The Capoque and Han insisted that the newcomers act as shamans, or medicine men, to cure those who were ill. Not knowing what to do, the Spaniards made the sign of the cross over the sick Indians, and prayed for them. To their surprise, some recovered. The Indians insisted that the Spanish medicine had worked, but it is more likely that their illness simply ran its course.

The dysentery took its toll on the Spanish party. Only 19 survived the winter, and some of those, including Cabeza de

Vaca, were still very ill when spring arrived. Any who were well enough went looking for New Spain. Estéban, Dorantes, and a third man, Alonso del Castillo, journeyed ahead to scout a trail for the others, but they were soon captured and enslaved by an unfriendly band of Indians. Still, their fate was luckier than that of their followers, who were killed somewhere along the coast.

Estéban, Dorantes, and Castillo stayed with their captors all summer, picking berries and carrying drinking water on an island surrounded by salt marshes. In August, Dorantes took a chance and swam away. Estéban left in November, and Castillo was right behind him.

Estéban and Castillo quickly met up with another tribe, the Iguace. They remained with the tribe for several years, learning its language and customs. In winter, they shared the Iguace meals of snakes, frogs, lizards, and rodents. In summer, they went north with the Indians to feast on the bright red fruit of the prickly pear cactus.

Native Americans from the coast and the plains liked to harvest prickly pears. Many tribes came together on the desert when the fruit was ripening, often putting aside disputes during the harvest. In the summer of 1532, Estéban was surprised to meet his old master, Dorantes, in the fields of cactus. Dorantes had been captured by another band of coastal Indians.

The two men met up again in the fall. This time, Estéban also saw Cabeza de Vaca. The treasurer of the ill-fated Narváez expedition had been traveling among the Indians as a trader. He had been on his way to New Spain when he was imprisoned by Dorantes's captors. Dorantes and Cabeza de Vaca whispered about escaping with Estéban and Castillo. But it was not until September 1534, when the tribes crossed paths again, that Dorantes and Cabeza de Vaca had a chance to slip away.

The four explorers now continued their long journey to New Spain. Following trails made by native people, they moved inland to avoid further capture along the coast. Now as they traveled, they were fortunate to meet tribes that greeted them in friendship and guided them on their journey.

Estében

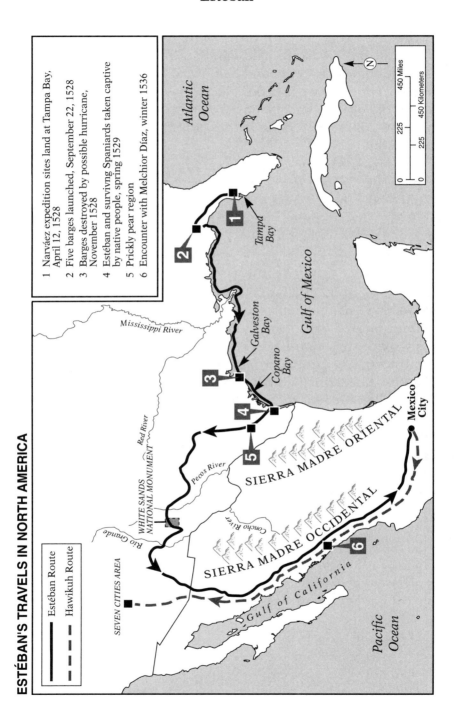

ESTÉBAN'S TRAVELS IN NORTH AMERICA

— Estében Route

- - - Hawikuh Route

1 Narváez expedition sites land at Tampa Bay, April 12, 1528
2 Five barges launched, September 22, 1528
3 Barges destroyed by possible hurricane, November 1528
4 Estében and surviving Spaniards taken captive by native people, spring 1529
5 Prickly pear region
6 Encounter with Melchior Díaz, winter 1536

Atlantic Ocean

Gulf of Mexico

Mississippi River

Galveston Bay

Copano Bay

Red River

WHITE SANDS NATIONAL MONUMENT

Rio Grande

Pecos River

SIERRA MADRE ORIENTAL

Mexico City

SEVEN CITIES AREA

Concho River

SIERRA MADRE OCCIDENTAL

Gulf of California

Pacific Ocean

450 Miles
225
450 Kilometers
225

They stayed for eight months with a group that Cabeza de Vaca called the Avavare. These Indians had seen the foreigners harvesting prickly pears and had heard of their power to cure illness. The Avavare asked their guests to remedy their headaches and other ailments. Castillo prayed over the ill as he and his companions had done before, and the Indians claimed to feel better.

The Spaniards wanted to appear superior to the Indians and rarely said a word to them. "It was the Negro who spoke to them all the time," wrote Cabeza de Vaca. "He asked about the trail we should follow, about the villages—in short, about everything we wished to know."

Estéban and his fellow travelers kept moving westward. Alongside the Colorado River, they met many native people fishing, hunting, and gathering berries. These people understood none of the Indian words Estéban had learned, so he communicated with them in sign language. The four wanderers were the first non-Indians to venture into many parts of the Southwest. The people of the region were curious about their visitors, especially Estéban, with his dark skin and curly hair. They called the four men Children of the Sun.

The explorers had many Indian guides to take them from one village to another. They were surprised to see the guides from each village rob the next one! The native people, in turn, were amazed at how the Children of the Sun could cover long distances while consuming small amounts of food. As Cabeza de Vaca explained, "We were, in reality, so used to hardships that we did not notice them any more."

In the foothills of a mountain range, a man gave Dorantes a copper rattle bearing the image of a human face. It came from a place to the west, he said, where many sheets of metal were buried in the ground. The explorers had heard that there were vast mineral deposits beside the Pacific Ocean. They reasoned that the coast must be near.

Then they crossed the mountains (the Sacramentos) and looked down on a large, white expanse that was not water, but sand. They probably saw the gypsum dunes that today make up White Sands National Monument in New Mexico. (The fact that the dunes are many miles from the Pacific Ocean shows that the men had no clear idea about where they were.) On the western side of the mountains, they heard about wealthy Indians living still farther west, in the Seven Cities of Cibola. Those Indians, it was said, possessed many jewels. They built tall houses and did not roam from place to place, as the nomadic tribes did.

The journey west took the four men across a desert so barren that they found nothing at all to eat. Beyond the desert, the explorers met a tribe with an ingenious method for cooking beans and squash. The Indians heated small stones over a fire, then dropped them into a hollow gourd that held water. When the hot stones made the water boil, the Indians added their food to it. They dropped in more hot stones to keep the water boiling.

Estéban and the Spaniards reached the land where the Pima Indians lived (in present-day Arizona). There, they saw people who lived in houses of grass and mud, and who used a system of ditches to irrigate their crops with river water. The Pima spoke about other Indians to the north who built houses several stories high and decorated them with green gems. Estéban and his fellow travelers exchanged knowing glances. The Seven Cities of Cibola must now lie to the north!

Yet instead of going north, they turned south, toward New Spain. Six hundred Pima accompanied them. The travelers began to see the burned villages and trampled fields that so often resulted from a Spanish encounter with Native Americans. They spotted an Indian wearing a piece of a Spanish belt and a horseshoe nail strung around his neck. Some Pima reported seeing thousands of Indians marching southward in chains, to work as slaves in Spanish mines.

After several days, the weary, naked survivors of the Narváez expedition happened upon four Spanish horsemen. Astonished at the story the explorers told, the horsemen took them to the town of Culiacán to meet Melchior Díaz, an official of the Spanish government.

Díaz fed and clothed his guests. He eyed their large Pima following, speculating that the Indians would make fine slaves. An enraged Cabeza de Vaca refused to see people he considered friends forced into slavery. He argued with Díaz and at last convinced him to send the Pima home.

Several Pima chose to remain with the Children of the Sun, however. They were with Estéban and his companions two months later, when they reached Mexico City, capital of the Spanish provinces in the Western Hemisphere. It was the spring of 1536. Estéban, Dorantes, Castillo, and Cabeza de Vaca had spent eight years traversing North America. They had covered 3,000 miles.

Of the four, only Cabeza de Vaca was of noble birth. So it was he who reported in person to the viceroy, Don Antonio de Mendoza, who was the king's representative in New Spain. All four of the travelers worked on a written account for the king. They told about the rivers, mountains, and deserts they had seen. They described varied wildlife, from the pronghorn antelopes that grazed on the open plain to the hard-skinned armadillos that burrowed quickly into the desert earth. Estéban supplied many details about the numerous tribes they had encountered.

The viceroy's eyes lit up when he heard about the Seven Cities of Cibola lying to the north. Francisco Pizarro recently had seized riches from the Inca in Peru. Perhaps, Mendoza thought, even greater wealth was waiting to be plundered.

In 1539, Mendoza asked Dorantes to lead an expedition going north, but Dorantes declined. Three years had passed, and his wandering days were over. Like Castillo, he had married and settled down in Mexico City. Cabeza de Vaca was on his way back to Spain, and so was unavailable as well.

Estéban, of course, was qualified to lead the expedition. He knew several Indian languages and had crossed the Southwest. But Mendoza hesitated to give so much responsibility to a black man. In the end, the viceroy put a priest, Father Marcos de Niza, in charge of the expedition. Estéban went along as a scout. It was his job to locate trails, food, and water. Estéban

A map of Mexico City from 1524.
(Rare Books and Manuscripts Division, The New York Public Library, Astor,
Lenox, and Tilden Foundations)

and Father Marcos began their journey on March 7, 1539, accompanied by another priest, Father Honoratus, a number of Indians, and an escort of soldiers.

Father Honoratus soon fell ill and turned back. And Father Marcos, who was not a young man, found the journey rough going as well. When the party reached a settlement called Vacapa, on Passion Sunday, two weeks before Easter, he decided to stay for the holiday. He sent Estéban and a group of Indians ahead with instructions. "I agreed with him that if he received any information of a rich, peopled land, that was something great, he should go no farther," Father Marcos wrote. The priest asked Estéban for a signal: "that if the thing was of moderate importance, he send me a white cross the size of a hand; if it was something great he send me one of two hands; and if it was something bigger and better than New Spain, he should send me a large cross."

Estéban left after dinner. Four days later, messengers returned carrying a cross "of the height of a man," Father Marcos reported. The messengers urged the priest to hurry along. Estéban had news of the Seven Cities of Cibola, they said. They spoke of a place where the people wore fine clothing and jewelry, where they built tall houses and adorned the porches with turquoise.

As exciting as this information was, Father Marcos waited to depart until after Easter. He expected Estéban to wait for him, but instead, the black explorer kept moving forward. The priest and his Native American guides followed a trail of white crosses Estéban left for them, and they slept at his abandoned campsites.

It was May when two Pima who had been with Estéban found Father Marcos on the trail. "They arrived covered with blood and with many wounds, and at their arrival they and those that were with me began such a weeping that from compassion and fear they made me cry also," the priest wrote.

The Pima said that upon approaching the first of the Seven Cities, Estéban gave them a gourd decorated with bells and feathers. He instructed them to show the gourd to the people of Cibola, and to announce his arrival.

In actuality, Estéban had reached not Cibola, but the Zuni Indian settlement Hawikuh. The Zuni lived in multistoried structures of dirt and mud called pueblos, and the Zuni women wore fine cotton robes, but the tribe possessed no riches. And instead of welcoming Estéban, they threw his gourd to the ground and told the Pima messengers he was forbidden to set foot in their city. An overconfident Estéban entered Hawikuh anyway. He and his Pima companions were immediately taken prisoner, and the Zuni elders met to discuss their fate.

Accounts differ about what happened next. The Pima who survived said that the Zuni shot arrows at them during an escape attempt, and that Estéban had been shot and killed. Some Zuni later said that they killed the black man because they feared he might be a spy or a sorcerer. There were also reports that Estéban left Hawikuh peacefully and settled alongside a river. The black explorer's true fate will never be known.

The news of Estéban's death frightened Father Marcos so much that he cut short his quest and hurried back to New Spain. But the story he told fueled curiosity and greed. Many people were now certain that gold and jewels abounded in the Seven Cities.

One person who heard the rumors was Francisco Vásquez de Coronado, governor of New Galicia, a frontier province in western Mexico. In 1540, he led an expedition of 230 soldiers, 800 Indian servants, and six priests toward the mythical Cibola. Coronado quickly took possession of Hawikuh by force. When he discovered no wealth, he moved on to explore the Colorado River and the Grand Canyon. There is evidence that he ventured into the southern plains as far as the Arkansas River. Coronado found no gold in the American Southwest, however, and the Spanish would not explore the region again for another 40 years.

For many years, most historians considered Coronado to be the principal explorer of the Southwest and the discoverer of

Hawikuh. They were reluctant to credit an African with such accomplishments. Although black scholars were writing about Estéban's travels as early as 1902, the few whites who were willing to acknowledge his contributions insisted he was an Arab, and not black at all!

With the growth of interest in African-American history in the second half of the 20th century, historians have taken a fresh look at the writings of Álvar Núñez Cabeza de Vaca and Father Marcos de Niza. They have concluded that Estéban was indeed a black man and the first to explore portions of the Southwest.

Chronology

▬▬▬▬▬▬▬

c. **1500**   The boy who would be named Estéban is born in the North African city of Azemmour

1527   sets sail for Florida with the Narváez expedition

1528   lands with the expedition at Tampa Bay; marches to Apalachen; sails toward New Spain; shipwrecked off Texas following a storm; taken in by the Capoque and Han Indians

1529   journeys again toward New Spain; captured by coastal Indians

1534   departs for New Spain with Castillo, Dorantes, and Cabeza de Vaca; begins a period of wandering and exploration in the American Southwest during which he hears stories of the Seven Cities of Cibola

1536   encounters Spanish horsemen at Culiacán; terminates journey in Mexico City

1539   serves as scout for an expedition in search of the Seven Cities of Cibola; enters the Zuni city Hawikuh; Estéban is presumed dead at the hands of the Zuni

Further Reading

Hallenbeck, Cleve. *Álvar Núñez, Cabeza de Vaca: The Journey and Route of the First European to Cross the Continent of North America.* 1970. Port Washington, N.Y.: Kennikat Press. A careful study of the travels of Estéban and his companions based on the writing of Cabeza de Vaca.

————. *The Journey of Fray Marcos de Niza.* 1987. Dallas: Southern Methodist University Press. Father Marcos's account of the 1539 expedition in search of the Seven Cities of Cibola.

Judge, Joseph. "Exploring Our Forgotten Century." *National Geographic,* March 1988. Unearthing artifacts of early Spanish settlement in the United States.

Logan, Rayford W. "Estevanico, Negro Discoverer of the Southwest: A Critical Reexamination." *Phylon,* Fourth Quarter 1940. A scholarly examination of 16th-century sources that establishes Estéban's race and explores the circumstances of his death.

Milanich, Jerald T., and Susan Milbrath, eds. *First Encounters: Spanish Explorations in the Caribbean and the United States, 1492–1570.* 1989. Gainesville, Fla.: University of Florida Press. A well-illustrated history of Spanish exploration in North America.

Shepherd, Elizabeth. *The Discoveries of Esteban the Black.* 1970. New York: Dodd, Mead, and Company. A biography for young readers.

Wright, Richard R. "Negro Companions of the Spanish Explorers." *Phylon,* Fourth Quarter 1941 (reprinted from the *American Anthropologist,* 1902). One of the first studies of the role of African Americans in exploring the New World.

Author's Note: Estéban is also referred to as Estevan, Estevanico, and Estevanillo in various resource materials. In this chapter I have used the preferred modern spelling of his name.

Jean-Baptiste Pointe du Sable
(*c.* 1745–1818)

*E*very day, elevated trains carry workers and tourists into "the Loop," the heart of downtown Chicago, Illinois. This is a bustling commercial center, a land of skyscrapers. Three of the nation's five tallest buildings are in Chicago. On warm days, the steel-and-glass towers form a sparkling backdrop for sunbathers on the shore of Lake Michigan.

Chicago is a hub of trade and transportation. Trucks and trains continually leave the city laden with produce and manufactured goods. Chicago serves as a connecting point in a great waterway, linking the Mississippi Valley with the Great Lakes and the St. Lawrence Seaway. The city's airport, O'Hare International, is the busiest in the United States.

Immigrants flocked to Chicago in the 19th and 20th centuries, and many Chicagoans still live in neighborhoods that reflect their Polish, German, Italian, Irish, Asian, or Mexican heritage. And the immigration continues: One seventh of the city's 3 million residents today are foreign born. African Americans make up 41 percent of Chicago's population. Most migrated to the city from farms in the South, or are the children or grandchildren of such migrants.

More than 200 years ago, an African-American trapper and trader paddled a canoe north through the wilderness to a plain alongside Lake Michigan. Jean-Baptiste Pointe du Sable built

17

a trading post in this lonely spot, and a community grew up around him. The city of Chicago now stands on the plain that he explored.

━━━━━━━━━━

In the early 1800s, Chief Black Partridge of the Potawatomi tribe entertained travelers on the Eschikagou Plain with stories of the past. "The first white man to settle at Eschikagou was a black man," he liked to say, "a quite black Frenchman named Jean-Baptiste Pointe du Sable."

Anything known today about Pointe du Sable's early life comes from similar recollections by people who knew him. Acquaintances of the black explorer recalled that he was born on the island of Hispaniola in the French colony of Saint-Domingue, which became the independent nation of Haiti in 1804. Pointe du Sable's father was said to be a French mariner, and his mother a black woman, the descendant of African slaves. Young Jean may have been educated in Paris like the sons of other prosperous families in Saint-Domingue. The fact that he valued literature and art backs up that claim. And he certainly was raised a Catholic. He remained devoted to the church throughout his life.

According to the old stories, Jean set sail from his island home when he became a man, seeking wealth and adventure on the North American mainland. France had claimed a large section of the continent, including the entire Mississippi River Valley. Pointe du Sable traveled with a friend, Jacques Clemorgan. Things went wrong for Jean and Jacques almost immediately, when they were shipwrecked off the coast of Louisiana during a storm. They made it to shore, but lost everything they owned. Luckily, the crew of a passing vessel spotted them and took them to New Orleans, the busy port near the mouth of the Mississippi River.

The French had founded New Orleans in 1718. From the city's docks, they shipped the bounty of the Mississippi and Ohio river valleys back to France. Sailing ships regularly left

New Orleans loaded with harvests of cotton and sugar cane, with timber, and especially with furs.

Beavers and other fur-bearing animals abounded in the North American wilderness, and Europeans could not get enough of their pelts. Beneath the long, protective outer hairs of its coat, the beaver has a layer of thick, velvety fur. Tiny barbs on this fur interlock when exposed to heat and pressure, forming a strong fabric, or felt. Europeans used the felt to make stylish hats.

The slave trade flourished in New Orleans as well, posing risks for a free black man, particularly one who had lost all of his money and identification. Jean feared that he would be captured and sold into slavery. He split up with Clemorgan and went to stay with a group of French priests who offered him shelter and work. He saved his earnings and bought a dugout canoe and supplies, so he could move north along the Mississippi River and into the wilderness, where he would be safer. He planned to support himself by trapping and trading with the Indians. Many native people of the Mississippi Valley trapped animals and traded the furs to Europeans for gunpowder, food, tools, and other items they wanted.

Jean-Baptiste Pointe du Sable paddled his dugout canoe 600 miles upriver to the small settlement of St. Louis. He spent several years on the river, and he developed a reputation for honesty among his Native American customers. The Indians had long had experience with other traders who shortchanged them or stuck them with shoddy goods. Through his business transactions, Pointe du Sable learned to communicate in the Indians' languages.

Many of the Native Americans Pointe du Sable befriended had fought on the French side in a series of wars with England. The largest of these was the French and Indian War, which began in 1754. With their Indian and colonial allies, France and England fought this war to decide once and for all who would dominate North America.

When the war ended officially with the Treaty of Paris (1763), Pointe du Sable was trading along the Mississippi River. The treaty gave the victorious British all French territory east of the Mississippi. France insisted that its territory west of the Mississippi, along with New Orleans, go to its ally Spain. The British were so glad to eliminate France from North America that they gave in to this demand with little argument.

Some time after 1770, Pointe du Sable moved on. He traveled north and east, following the course of the Illinois River. After several weeks, he came to a flat expanse of land where violets, buttercups, and wild garlic and onions grew. The Indians of the region called the spot Eschikagou, a name that referred to the scent of garlic in the air.

The river journey brought Pointe du Sable close to the shore of Lake Michigan. He hiked over to the water's edge and felt a thrill of excitement. The Eschikagou Plain, he saw, was an important portage, or overland route, connecting the Great Lakes with the Mississippi and its tributaries to form an inland waterway. Here was a route that could carry people and goods from the mouth of the St. Lawrence River, on the Atlantic coast, to the southern port of New Orleans, more than a thousand miles from where he stood.

The Eschikagou Plain belonged to the Potawatomi, people who lived in bark-covered longhouses sheltering eight to ten families. The Potawatomi cultivated maize and pumpkins. They played lacrosse for fun, but the games between villages could be rough and competitive. Many players were injured by swinging bats or by the swiftly moving ball of solid wood.

Pointe du Sable knew enough of the Potawatomi language to greet them in friendship and secure their permission to hunt and trap on the Eschikagou Plain. The furs from the region were unusually fine and brought a high price on the market in St. Louis. But a strong, frigid wind blew across the plain in winter, so when Pointe du Sable built his first cabin at Eschikagou, he chose a spot to the south, on the Illinois River.

The Potawatomi soon adopted the friendly trader into their tribe. In an Indian ceremony, Pointe du Sable married Catherine, a Potawatomi woman. Catherine had been named for an ancestor who was baptized by the "Black Robes," 17th-century

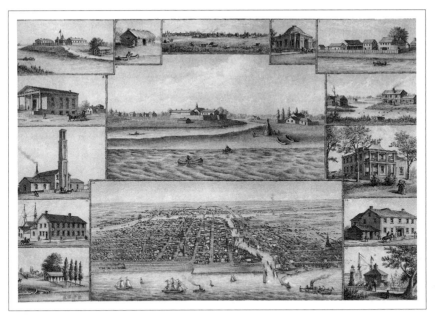

*This antique print shows scenes from Chicago's founding and development.
In the second box from the left, at the top, Jean-Baptiste Pointe du Sable
paddles a canoe past his log cabin.*
(Library of Congress)

French missionaries who had ventured into the wilderness to
convert the native people to Catholicism.

In 1776, war broke out again in North America. This time,
England's 13 American colonies fought for independence. The
war brought a new group of settlers to Eschikagou. They were
French families from Quebec who hoped to distance themselves from their English rulers. England had denied the Canadians basic rights, such as the freedom to assemble. Now,
England was taxing the Canadians to support the war with the
colonies.

The British took a beating in the East. On Christmas night,
1776, General George Washington and his troops crossed the
Delaware to surprise a force of Hessians—German soldiers
fighting for England—at Trenton, New Jersey. Nine days later,

Washington struck at Princeton, New Jersey, forcing the British general Lord Cornwallis and his soldiers to retreat to New York. American victories in two battles at Saratoga, New York, in September and October 1777, ended a British plan to divide the colonies in two. They forced General John Burgoyne of the British army to surrender his troops. The American successes had another beneficial result: They induced France to join the war against England.

The British still held on strongly west of the Appalachians, though. They manned several forts in the region and had formed an alliance with some of the Indians.

Jean-Baptiste Pointe du Sable left no record of his thoughts about the war, but he aroused the suspicions of Colonel Arent Schuyler de Peyster, the commander of Fort Michilimackinac, an English outpost on Lake Huron. De Peyster informed his superiors in New York City that "Jean-Baptiste Pointe du Sable, is a handsome Negro, well educated, and settled in trade at Eschikagou. However, he is much in the French interest." Pointe du Sable's fluency in French, the language of England's longtime enemy, caused de Peyster to mistrust him.

In the summer of 1779, de Peyster's men tracked the African American to a creekside cabin in present-day Indiana. A Lieutenant Bennett arrested Pointe du Sable, confiscated the goods in his possession, and locked him up at Fort Michilimackinac. Pointe du Sable, though innocent, was a model prisoner. "The Negro since his imprisonment has in every respect behaved as became a man in his situation, and has many friends, who give him a good character," Bennett stated in a report. With no evidence that Pointe du Sable had engaged in any wrongdoing, de Peyster soon let him go.

Curiously, it turned out that at the time of his arrest, the trader who was said to be "in the French interest" had been doing business with an Englishman named Durand. An angry Durand filed a claim with the British government for the items that had been confiscated, which he said belonged to him. He billed his government for 500 pounds of flour, 220 pounds of pork, four bear skins, a canoe decorated with plumes, and other goods.

Pointe du Sable went back to his trading post at Eschikagou and built a sturdier home on the plain, at the sandy spot where the Eschikagou (now the Chicago) River flows into Lake Michigan. He fashioned the walls of his new cabin of logs cut from the forest surrounding the flat land, and cleared several acres for planting. His mind filled with plans, he constructed a lodging house for travelers and a trading post on the Eschikagou River. The number of people moving west was increasing. Pointe du Sable wanted to provide them with a place to stop and rest as well as with food, clothing, blankets, tools, and cooking utensils. He ordered the goods for his trading post from a merchant named Thomas Smith in Detroit. Located 275 miles east of Eschikagou, Detroit was the largest town west of the Appalachians and the site of a British fort. Smith's ledgers show that he did business with Jean-Baptiste Pointe du Sable until April 16, 1783.

General Cornwallis surrendered to George Washington at Yorktown, Virginia, on October 19, 1781, following the final confrontation of the Revolutionary War. The former colonies were now an independent nation, the United States of America, with control of all land south of Canada and east of the Mississippi River, a region that included Eschikagou.

A small community quickly grew up in the newly American settlement at Eschikagou. Jean and Catherine now had a son, Jean, and a daughter, Suzanne. Pointe du Sable's holdings soon included a bakery, a dairy, a smokehouse, chicken coops, barns, and a stable. He purchased furniture, china, books, and paintings for his home from Quebec. Increasing numbers of people passed over the portage every year. Pointe du Sable built docks on Lake Michigan and cleared a road to carry travelers from the lake to the river. At times he traveled the waterways himself, bringing supplies to settlers at their homesteads.

Yet as the village prospered, its founder grew restless. He bought 30 acres of farmland at Peoria, on the Illinois River, where his old friend Jacques Clemorgan lived. Jean and

Catherine traveled to St. Louis in 1788, and were married again in a Catholic ceremony. St. Louis in the 1780s looked much different from the trappers' outpost that Pointe du Sable had known in the 1760s. It was now a town covering 3 square miles, with restaurants, shops, and wooden sidewalks. St. Louis even had a theater.

In 1796, Pointe du Sable sold his property at Eschikagou to a French trader named Joseph le Mai and moved with his family to Peoria, where young Jean opened a trading post. Suzanne had married, and Jean and Catherine watched her children grow up.

Eschikagou underwent many changes after Pointe du Sable left. Its name evolved to Checagou, and then to Chicago. Joseph le Mai sold the Pointe du Sable property to a Canadian of Scottish descent, John Kinzie, in 1804. Soon afterward, the United States constructed a military post on the plain. Called Fort Dearborn, it would be the site of an Indian attack in which many soldiers and settlers would die during the War of 1812. (In that war, Indians, desperate to regain some of their land from the Americans, fought on the side of the British.)

Catherine died in the early 1800s, and Jean went to live with his married granddaughter, Eulalie de Roi, in St. Charles, Missouri. He died on August 29, 1818, at the approximate age of 73, and was buried in a St. Charles cemetery following a funeral Mass.

In the years following his death, a city rose on the shore of Lake Michigan. In 1837, the year Chicago was incorporated, its population had reached 4,000. A railroad came to the city in the late 1840s. The early Chicagoans honored the trader John Kinzie as their city's founder, and the name of Jean-Baptiste Pointe du Sable was largely forgotten.

Then, early in the 20th century, scholars began to look more closely at historical documents from the days of western exploration and settlement. They examined letters from people such as Colonel de Peyster, the records of Thomas Smith of Detroit and other merchants, and personal memoirs, such as the writings of Juliette Kinzie, wife of John

Jean-Baptiste Pointe du Sable

*In 1831, Fort Dearborn dominated the settlement on the Eschikagou Plain.
To the right are the buildings purchased by John Kinzie that originally
belonged to Pointe du Sable.*
(Library of Congress)

Kinzie. They discovered that Jean-Baptiste Pointe du Sable had
settled at Eschikagou at least 25 years before John Kinzie!

In 1912, the Chicago Historical Society placed a plaque on a
soap factory at the corner of Pine and Kinzie streets. The plaque
commemorated the "Site of the first house in Chicago. Erected
about 1779 by Jean-Baptiste Pointe du Sable, a Negro from
Santo Domingo." The people of Chicago have since named a
high school and a museum of African-American history for
their city's first resident. Jean-Baptiste Pointe du Sable is now
recognized as a key figure in Chicago's history.

Chronology

c. 1745	Jean-Baptiste Pointe du Sable born in Saint-Domingue (later Haiti, on the island of Hispaniola)
the early 1760s	arrives in New Orleans; becomes a trapper and trader on the Mississippi River
1763	the treaty ending the French and Indian War gives French territory east of the Mississippi River to Britain
the early 1770s	Pointe du Sable comes to Eschikagou; is adopted by the Potawatomi; marries Catherine in an Indian ceremony
1776	the American colonies declare their independence from England; the Revolutionary War begins
1779	Pointe du Sable arrested and imprisoned at Fort Michilimackinac; builds a new cabin at Eschikagou
1781	Americans achieve victory in the revolution; the United States of America is born
1788	Jean and Catherine are married in a Catholic ceremony at St. Louis
1796	Pointe du Sable sells his property at Eschikagou; retires to Peoria
1818	Pointe du Sable dies

Further Reading

African Americans, Voices of Triumph: Perseverance. 1993. Alexandria, Va.: Time-Life Books. A short description of Pointe du Sable's coming to Eschikagou.

Gibb, C. R. *Black Explorers.* 1992. Silver Spring, Md.: Three Dimensional Publishing Co. A summary of Pointe du Sable's life and accomplishments in a chapter on "African Exploration of the Americas."

Logan, Rayford W., and Michael R. Winston, eds. *Dictionary of American Negro Biography.* 1982. New York: W. W. Norton and Company. A brief review of Pointe du Sable's life and contributions.

Author's note: In researching this chapter, I turned to the following old sources. These books may be available in university libraries or special collections. Readers can compare them to see how the story of Pointe du Sable changed as information was uncovered.

Gilbert, Paul Thomas, and Charles Lee Bryson. *Chicago and Its Makers.* Chicago: Felix Mendelsohn, 1929. A large book on Chicago's development.

Matlock-Simon, Elizabeth, and Hubert V. Simon. *Chicago's First Citizen—Jean Baptiste Pointe De Sable.* 1933. Chicago: Elizabeth Matlock-Simon and Hubert V. Simon Co. A pamphlet that accurately summarizes Pointe du Sable's life and the existing historical evidence.

Quaife, Milo Milton. *Checagou: From Indian Wigwam to Modern City.* 1933. Chicago: University of Chicago Press.

———. *Chicago and the Old Northwest, 1673–1835.* 1913. Chicago: University of Chicago Press. Quaife's two books discuss what was known about Pointe du Sable at the time of their publication.

James Beckwourth
(1800–1866)

James Beckwourth in a daguerreotype, circa 1855.
(Nevada Historical Society)

---

*B*etween 1840 and 1860, 300,000 people headed for the "land of opportunity." They crossed the Great Plains to settle in the Far West. Most of these pioneers dreamed of finding a better life. "But the particular means by which each proposed to attain this end," said Jesse Quinn Thornton, who found a new home in Oregon, "were as various as can be imagined."

Many migrants sought fertile land and a mild climate for farming. Others, such as the Mormons who journeyed to Utah, wanted religious freedom. Some people went west in search of riches. They swarmed to California during the Gold Rush of 1849. Dreams of gold and silver brought thousands to Nevada a decade later.

Pioneer families packed their belongings in covered wagons and crossed a vast western landscape that was only partly explored. They stuck to trails named for their destinations: Santa Fe, Oregon, California.

Two thirds of all travelers moving west went to California. They picked up the Oregon Trail in Independence, Missouri and followed it over the plains to Fort Laramie, an army outpost in Wyoming. With oxen or mules pulling their wagons, they were lucky to cover 15 miles in a day. The entire trip would take four and a half months.

There were few trading posts along the Oregon Trail. Families that ran out of food killed and ate their oxen. There were no doctors to treat the sick. Nearly all of the 20,000 people who died on the trails succumbed to cholera, diphtheria, and other diseases. Pioneers commonly fell victim to white outlaws who roamed the plains. (The native tribes, although greatly feared, rarely attacked wagon trains.)

After resting and buying supplies at Fort Laramie, the migrants drove their wagons up into the Rocky Mountains. The steep climb was hard work for both people and animals.

The California Trail branched south from the Oregon Trail at the Raft River in Idaho. California-bound travelers had to cross the Great Basin, in Utah. This desert of hard-baked clay and white salt sand covers 200,000 square miles. One woman who crossed the parching expanse complained of being "obliged to swallow dust all day instead of water."

At last, only the Sierra Nevada lay between the weary pioneers and their destination. Many people who went to California in the 1850s remembered a vibrant, talkative man who led them across the mountain range. He was Jim Beckwourth—explorer, adventurer, and legend in his own lifetime. Beckwourth had discovered a pass through the Sierra Nevada, a route that eased the way into California. Thousands of settlers used Beckwourth Pass to reach their new home.

The details of James Pierson Beckwourth's early life are obscure. Historians believe he was born in 1800, in Frederick County, Virginia. He is thought to have been the son of Jennings Beckwith, a white man from a prominent family who fought in the American Revolution. Nothing is known about James Beckwourth's mother, except that she was a black woman and a slave.

By 1809, Jennings Beckwith had moved with his slaves to the edge of the frontier. He settled in St. Charles, Louisiana Territory, near the junction of the Missouri and Mississippi rivers. St. Charles was the town in which Jean-Baptiste Pointe du Sable would spend his final years.

Young Jim grew up in a "howling wilderness," he said. It was a wild, forested region, where the neighboring families built a stockade as protection from the local Indians. The Native Americans resented the settlers who encroached on their land and had been known to attack without warning.

Jim attended school for a few years on the frontier. It was unusual for a slave to receive schooling, and this fact is evidence that Jennings Beckwith cared deeply for his son. When he was 19, Jim went to the nearby town of St. Louis to be an apprentice to a blacksmith. "I felt myself already quite a man," he recalled. But in St. Louis, Jim paid more attention to a young woman he had met than to his work. He stayed out late at night and angered his boss. Arguments erupted, and soon the blacksmith sent the cocky apprentice back to his father.

Jim was restless at home. Explorers and traders were opening up the land to the west. Jim heard stories of tall mountain ranges, wild rivers, and vast deserts. He longed to see those sights for himself. He craved action and adventure. Most of all, he desired renown—he wanted people in the East and the West to learn of his deeds.

James Beckwourth

In 1822, Jim Beckwourth traveled up the Mississippi River as part of an expedition led by Colonel Richard M. Johnson of the United States Army. The group was headed for the Fever River in what is now Illinois. The Fever River region held rich deposits of lead. The U.S. government sought an agreement with the Indians that would allow Americans to mine the dull, grayish metal.

While the officers met with the Indian leaders, Jim visited the mining town of Galena. He had to climb a ladder up the muddy riverbank to reach the town. The 74 residents of Galena lived in tents and cabins in summer. In winter, they moved into abandoned mine shafts to stay warm.

The young African American enjoyed meeting the area's Indians. "The Indians soon became very friendly to me, and I was indebted to them for showing me their choicest hunting grounds," he said. Jim spent 18 months alongside the Fever River, hunting and mining for lead. The money he earned made him feel like "quite a wealthy personage," he remarked.

In the summer of 1824, when General William Ashley was planning a fur-trading expedition, Jim Beckwourth signed on as a recruit. Beckwourth was "possessed by a strong desire to see the celebrated Rocky Mountains, and the great Western Wilderness so much talked about," he said. Before Jim left, Jennings Beckwith signed a deed of emancipation, a document releasing his son from slavery. Jim Beckwourth was now officially a free man.

Ashley, Beckwourth, and their companions made their way to the Platte River in the present state of Nebraska. A party of 26 men waited for them there, hungry and discouraged. "They had been expecting the arrival of a large company with abundant supplies, and when we joined them without any provisions, they were greatly disappointed," Jim recalled.

General Ashley sent out the best hunters to bring in some game. At the same time, Jim Beckwourth grabbed his rifle and went out alone. He soon shot a duck. But his appetite got the best of him, and he cooked and ate it on the spot. Just as he swallowed the last mouthful, Beckwourth thought of the hungry men and felt ashamed of his selfishness. From then on, he said, he "never refused to share my last shilling, my last biscuit, or my only blanket with a friend. . . ."

Determined now to feed the others, Beckwourth tracked down and killed a deer and three elk. And when the game was brought into camp, he boasted, "the fame of 'Jim Beckwourth' was celebrated by all tongues."

That autumn, Ashley's men moved west toward the Laramie Plains. Beckwourth saw much of the scenery he had heard about for so long. He saw swift rivers, deep canyons, and herds of buffalo that stretched to the horizon.

Winter brought powerful storms to the plains. Some nights, the men slept on the ground. They burned all of their firewood and consumed all of their food. If it were not for the Pawnee Loup Indians, Beckwourth and the others might have died. The tribe sheltered the trappers in their lodges. They fed the men and their horses.

Later, Beckwourth enjoyed telling stories about his adventures with the Ashley party to anyone who would listen. He could not resist playing with the facts, though, and soon earned a reputation as a "gaudy liar." For example, he liked to describe the time he pulled General Ashley from the Green River. The general indeed had been saved from drowning, but by someone else. Beckwourth had been in a boat on a distant part of the river when the rescue occurred.

Trappers, soldiers, and mountain men passed along Beckwourth's stories as they sat around campfires and visited forts and Indian villages. Soon, people who had never met Beckwourth knew his name. The Crow Indians were sure he was a member of their tribe who had been stolen in childhood!

This belief worked to Beckwourth's advantage when Crow warriors captured him in 1826. He feared he would be killed. Instead, he said, "I was being hugged and kissed to death by a whole lodge of near and dear Crow relatives. . . ."

The Crow, who numbered more than 7,000, lived in two main groups. They were a nomadic tribe that followed the buffalo herds. Immediately, they accepted Beckwourth as one of their own. He fought in battles against the Blackfoot tribe, enemies of the Crow. His bravery brought him stature, allowing him to join the tribal council, the Crow governing body.

Beckwourth lived for nearly ten years as a Crow. They were years filled with adventure. "I had traversed the fastnesses of the far Rocky Mountains in summer heats and winter frosts," he said. "I had encountered savage beasts and wild men."

In 1836, Beckwourth left the tribe and made his way back to St. Louis. He hoped to join a fur-trading expedition, but the western fur trade was tapering off. He heard about a job opportunity in Florida, where the army was fighting the Seminole Indians.

The United States wanted the Seminole to give up their land in Florida and move to the Indian Territory (now Oklahoma). But the Seminole stood their ground. The army then planned to move the Seminole by force or wipe them out, and bloody battles took place. The Seminole used their knowledge of the wilderness to hide from the U.S. forces.

President Martin Van Buren called for western mountain men to aid in the war. Adept in Indian ways and warfare, they would be helpful to the army, Van Buren believed. For Jim, the Seminole Wars were a way to gain renown.

Jim Beckwourth went to Florida as a civilian employee of the army, although he called himself "Captain." He broke in mules for the soldiers, drove wagons, and carried messages between the commanders and their troops in the field.

He also saw combat. On December 7, 1837, the soldiers and Indians fought the Battle of Okeechobee, just north of the Everglades. An experienced Indian fighter, Beckwourth quickly saw that the Seminole had the advantage. "The spot was thickly overgrown with trees, and a number of our assailants were concealed among the branches," he observed. In hiding, the Seminole aimed their rifles at the soldiers. They killed or wounded many men.

The American officers claimed victory at Okeechobee and asked Beckwourth to carry the news to their commanders. "I could not see that O-ke-cho-be was much of a victory,"

Beckwourth commented years later. "But it was called a victory by the soldiers and they were the best qualified to decide."

By 1842, the war in Florida was over. Most of the Seminole had agreed to move west. The few who stayed behind retreated to the swampland of the Everglades. Beckwourth was now back on the frontier, having left Florida when he saw little chance there for renown.

Over the next few years, it seemed that if something exciting happened in the West, Jim Beckwourth was a part of it. When the United States went to war with Mexico in 1846, he acted as a guide and messenger for the army. The Americans started this controversial war to gain lands under Mexican rule. Beckwourth was present when U.S. forces captured the settlement of Santa Fe, New Mexico. He opened a hotel in Santa Fe that became a favorite spot for drink and entertainment among officers and enlisted men.

The Mexican War ended on February 2, 1848, with the Treaty of Guadalupe Hidalgo. The treaty established the border of Texas at the Rio Grande. Mexico ceded California and New Mexico to the United States.

Just days before the signing of the treaty, gold was discovered in northern California. News of the find traveled slowly, reaching the East Coast in August. The news filtered north to Oregon and south to Mexico, Peru, and Chile. People with "gold fever" hurried to California by the thousands.

Beckwourth saw the Gold Rush as a business opportunity. He traveled throughout the mining region selling clothing to the prospectors. He eventually settled down in the new town of Sonora, California and opened a small store. At night, he set up tables for gambling under the awning in front of his shop. The prospectors liked to wager their newfound riches on games of cards and chance. These games earned Beckwourth thousands of dollars—much more money than he needed. He was known to treat the entire population of Sonora to drinks and celebrations.

But even riches could not keep Beckwourth in one place for long. He left Sonora in 1850. "Inactivity fatigued me to death," he explained. He went north to look for gold.

In the spring of that year, while he and a friend were prospecting near the Pit River, he noticed what he thought could be a pass through the mountains. It seemed to Beckwourth that settlers might enter California more easily through this pass than through the ones they were then using. Not wanting someone else to take credit for his find, he kept his observation to himself. He planned to come back and explore the pass at a later date.

His chance came soon after, when he went prospecting with 12 other men. "We proceeded in an easterly direction and all busied themselves in searching for gold," he said, "but my errand was of a different character: I had come to discover what I suspected to be a pass."

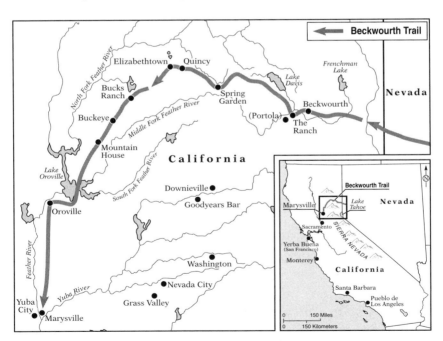

The Beckwourth Trail

Marysville, California, the end of the journey for many pioneers traveling through Beckwourth Pass.
(Yuba County Library, California)

The route Beckwourth found would shorten the pioneers' journey by 150 miles. It was the lowest pass through the Sierra Nevada north of the Mojave Desert.

Beckwourth and the 12 prospectors entered a meadow near the pass, at the northwest extremity of the mountain range. "This," Beckwourth observed, "would afford the best wagon-road into the American Valley."

Excitedly, Beckwourth told three trusted friends about his discovery. The four were soon at work clearing a road through the pass and the valley. Word of Beckwourth's find got around. The publisher of the Marysville, California newspaper proclaimed, "This route is by far the most important to the emigration and valuable to our city, taking into consideration the distances involved and the advantages of the road."

By the middle of the summer of 1851, the trail was ready. Beckwourth, splendid in Indian attire, led the first wagon train through the pass and across the valley.

Ina Coolbrith, a California poet, rode through Beckwourth Pass in 1851, when she traveled west as a child. "We were guided by the famous scout, Jim Beckwourth, who was an historical figure," she recalled, "and one of the most beautiful creatures that ever lived. He was rather dark and wore his hair in two long braids, twisted with colored cord that gave him a picturesque appearance. He wore a leather coat and moccasins and rode a horse without a saddle."

Beckwourth invited Ina and her sister to ride with him on his horse. "I was the happiest little girl in the world," Ina Coolbrith said. After a long ride, the travelers reached a spot in the mountains where they could look down and see their destination. Beckwourth stopped his horse and pointed. "Here is California, little girls," he said, "here is your kingdom."

The pioneers nearing the end of their journey were a tired, ragged group. Beckwourth saw many wagons with torn covers, with wheels held on by ropes and rags. He saw people whose shoes had worn away, whose clothing was ripped and dirty. In 1852, he went back into the hotel business. He opened an inn and trading post in the valley adjacent to Beckwourth Pass. There, at "the emigrant's landing place," he offered hot meals and kindness.

A pioneer named Granville Stuart remembered that "His nature was a hospitable and generous one, and he supplied the pressing necessities of starving emigrants, often without money—they agreeing to pay him later, which I regret to say, a number of them failed to do."

Beckwourth had never forgotten his promise to himself to share whatever he had. "I can not find it in my heart to refuse relief to such necessities, and, if my pocket suffers a little, I have my recompense in a feeling of internal satisfaction," he stated.

In 1854, Beckwourth dictated his autobiography to T. D. Bonner, a justice of the peace. *The Life and Adventures of James*

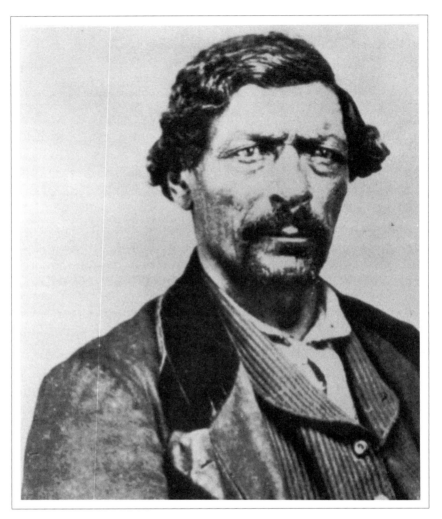

Jim Beckwourth in the 1860s.
(Nevada Historical Society)

P. *Beckwourth,* published two years later, allowed readers to thrill to Beckwourth's deeds, both real and exaggerated. The book brought greater renown, but it made little difference in Beckwourth's life. He planted a garden outside his hotel, and he kept cattle and mules.

James Beckwourth

No one knows why Jim Beckwourth left California in 1858. According to one story, he lost everything he owned in a bet. Other people said he had been wrongly blamed for stealing horses from his neighbors. It may be that he simply decided to pull up his roots once more.

At age 58, he opened a store in Denver, Colorado, selling everything from fine china to wines to winter clothing. As Western towns grew more settled, people demanded the goods that had been available to them in the East. And Beckwourth still went out hunting and trapping. He was the lone survivor of an 1860 trapping expedition on Utah's Green River. The other members drowned or were killed by Indians.

Jim Beckwourth died in 1866, while leading a peacemaking mission to the Crow tribe, the people with whom he had lived as a young man. The cause of his death was a matter of controversy among 19th-century historians and remains so today. Some historians believed a rumor that the Crow had poisoned Beckwourth to keep him from leaving again. Supposedly, the Crow were determined to have Beckwourth in death if they could not have him in life.

Others believed Lieutenant George Templeton of the U.S. Army, who was with Beckwourth at the end of his life, and who told a different story. The black explorer had been feeling ill before the tribal visit, Templeton said, and had died of natural causes in the Crow village. "I was very sorry to hear of his death as he was a very pleasant man," Templeton wrote in his diary. "He was, with all his faults, certainly a man of some talent, and was what might be called decidedly smart."

Chronology

1800	James Pierson Beckwourth born in Frederick County, Virginia
1809	moves to Louisiana Territory
1819	serves as an apprentice to a St. Louis blacksmith
1822	travels to Galena, on the Fever River, with a U.S. Army expedition
1824	Beckwourth is granted his freedom; joins the Ashley Expedition
1826	captured by the Crow; accepted as a member of their tribe
1836	travels to Florida to assist the army in its war with the Seminole
1846	serves as a guide and messenger for the army during the Mexican War; opens a hotel in Santa Fe, New Mexico
1849	journeys to California; earns his living by trading with prospectors
1850	becomes a prospector himself; discovers a pass through the Sierra Nevada
1851	begins leading wagon trains through Beckwourth Pass
1852	opens an inn and trading post to serve pioneers
1856	Beckwourth's autobiography is published
1858	Beckwourth leaves California; opens a store in Denver, Colorado
1860	survives a disastrous trapping expedition on the Green River in Utah
1866	returns to the Crow to make peace on behalf of the U.S. government; Jim Beckwourth dies

Further Reading

African Americans, Voices of Triumph: Perseverance. 1993. Alexandria, Va.: Time-Life Books. Contains two pages describing the life of James Beckwourth.

Altman, Susan. *Extraordinary Black Americans from Colonial to Contemporary Times.* 1989. Chicago: Children's Press. Includes a short section on Beckwourth's career.

Bonner, T. D. *The Life and Adventures of James P. Beckwourth, Mountaineer, Scout, Pioneer and Chief of the Crow Nation.* 1965. Minneapolis: Ross and Haines, Inc. A reprint of the autobiography that Beckwourth dictated to T. D. Bonner in the 1850s.

Gibb, C. R. *Black Explorers.* 1992. Silver Spring, Md.: Three Dimensional Publishing. Describes Beckwourth's life and accomplishments.

The Pioneers. 1974. Alexandria, Va.: Time-Life Books. A lively, illustrated account of western migration in the 19th century.

Wilson, Elinor. *Jim Beckwourth: Black Mountain Man and War Chief of the Crows.* 1972. Norman, Okla.: University of Oklahoma Press. A scholarly biography of Beckwourth that separates fact from legend.

Charles Young
(1864–1922)

Charles Young.
(Library of Congress)

*C*hristmas Day, 1912, was as hot and humid as any other day in the thick jungle of Liberia. A hundred soldiers crouched in leafy hiding places while monkeys called to one another in the branches overhead. The soldiers were Liberian, but they took orders from an American, Major Charles Young of the United States Army.

Young was the American military attaché assigned to Liberia. It was his job to advise the American ambassador in that country on military matters. President D. E. Howard of Liberia, however, had asked Young to lead a dangerous mission. The president wanted Young to rescue a Liberian officer, Captain Browne, and his unit of 78 men who were surrounded by angry members of the Gola tribe.

The West African nation of Liberia was established in the mid-19th century by freed American slaves. The settlers, known as Americo-Liberians, lived mostly on the Atlantic coast. Their nation's history had been marked by frequent disputes with the native people of the interior.

Young and his soldiers waited and listened, keeping as silent as possible. It had been 30 days since they had left the capital of Monrovia, and now they were lost and low on ammunition. They feared they were in the territory of the Manos people, who were rumored to eat their enemies' flesh. A careless noise picked up by the wrong ears could mean death.

Major Young crept out of hiding and scouted the area. He determined that it was safe for his force to move on. On December 29, at a place called Tappi, the military unit at last located Captain Browne and his men, who were fending off armed Gola tribesmen. Young ordered his soldiers into action. The battle was intense, and Young was wounded in his right arm. But soon the attackers were driven off, and Young led the soldiers—both rescuers and rescued—back to Monrovia, where he received grateful praise from President Howard.

The journey into the jungle was more than a military mission for Charles Young. It was an exploratory trip as well. All the way to Tappi and back, he made notes about the forests and marshes he traversed. He jotted down ideas about the potential for growing rice and cocoa in the region. He sketched maps, all the while looking for places where roads might be built. As he crossed wide rivers that were home to pygmy hippopotamuses, he envisioned bridges connecting the shores.

The information he collected was of great value to the Liberian government in developing their nation. The Liberian secretary of state wrote to the U.S. State Department to convey his government's "grateful appreciation for the most valuable services rendered the Republic by Major Young."

———————

Charles Young was born in a log cabin on a Mays Lick, Kentucky plantation on March 12, 1864, three years into the Civil War. Kentucky was one of the "border states"—that is, one of four Union states bordering the Confederacy in which slavery was allowed. In fact, Charles's parents, Armintie and Gabriel Young, were slaves.

It was a turbulent time. Thousands had died in the war, and the armies of the North and the South needed men. The Union army promised freedom to any slave who enlisted. So before Charles was a year old, Gabriel Young signed on as a private in Company F, 5th Regiment of Colored Artillers. African Americans in the Civil War served in segregated units under the command of white officers.

After his discharge from the army in February 1866, Gabriel returned to Kentucky. Armintie, little Charles, and all of the slaves in every state were now free. The Youngs and some of their relatives left the plantation and moved across the Ohio River to Ripley, Ohio.

Charles's grandmother was determined that the boy would be well educated. She helped him with his lessons while he was in grammar school. He went on to earn high grades at Ripley High School, and to graduate with honors. In 1882, he returned to his grammar school to teach under the direction of his old principal, Dr. J. T. Whitson.

One day, a notice in the Ripley newspaper caught Dr. Whitson's eye. The announcement stated that young men who wanted to become military academy cadets could take a qualifying test in the town of Hillsboro, Ohio. The United States Military Academy at West Point, New York trains its cadets to be army officers.

Charles Young

Immediately, Whitson thought of Charles. He showed the notice to his former pupil and urged him to take the examination. All of Charles Young's study and hard work was about to pay off. He took the qualifying exam and received the second-highest score. Young was officially accepted by the military academy on May 20, 1884.

Only a few African Americans had attended West Point before Charles Young. All had endured insults and cruel treatment from the white cadets. Young was no exception. The other cadets called him a "load of coal." They excluded him from their social activities. No white classmate would chat with him or be his friend. "He had no comrades at the academy," recalled Major General Charles D. Rhodes, who had attended West Point with Young. "I remember him conversing in German with some foreign-born shoe-blacks and my reaction was that sheer loneliness impelled him to converse with anyone who took an interest in his conversation."

Young refused to be discouraged by the racism he endured. After five years of lonely hard work, he completed the academy's tough curriculum. Through his example, he dispelled some of the prejudice against him. "In time, some of the outstanding cadets came to admire Young's perseverance and treat him with the kindness that had long been his due," Major General Rhodes wrote.

On August 31, 1889, Charles Young became the third African American to graduate from West Point. Henry Flipper, the first black graduate, left the academy in 1877. He was later accused of mishandling government funds and was dishonorably discharged from the army. Flipper insisted he was the victim of a racist plot, and Congress at last cleared his record in 1976, 36 years after his death. John Alexander, another African American, graduated from the academy in 1887. Sadly, he died of a heart attack after seven years of military service.

Like many career army officers, Lieutenant Charles Young moved from one assignment to another. He began his service on the western frontier with the 9th Cavalry, a black regiment of soldiers on horseback. The 9th Cavalry was one of four black

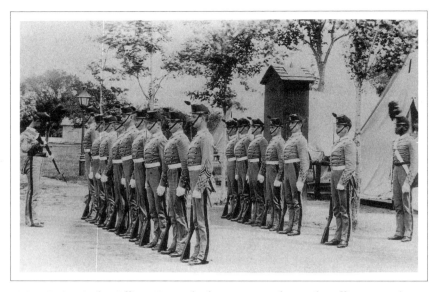

West Point Cadet Officer Young looks on as another cadet officer completes an inspection of arms.
(U.S. Army Military History Institute)

army regiments, nicknamed Buffalo Soldiers, that helped keep peace between settlers and Indians in the West.

The rest of the regiment's officers were white, and Young endured loneliness at his western posts, just as he had at West Point. According to an efficiency report from Fort Du Chesne, Utah, where Young served between 1890 and 1894, the black lieutenant was "liked and respected but very much alone socially."

Although West Point graduates are trained to be leaders, the army often was at a loss about what to do with a black officer. To let him give orders to white subordinates seemed unthinkable! In the years ahead, Young would be stationed in the Philippines and in Mexico with the 9th Cavalry. He would act as superintendent of two national parks in California.

In 1894, Young was assigned to teach military history at Wilberforce University, a college for African Americans in

Ohio. He would have preferred to lead soldiers, but he took on his teaching duties cheerfully, even pitching in to teach French and mathematics classes. (He had a talent for languages and had mastered Italian, Spanish, Latin, and Greek as well as French and German.) Young was "thoroughly loyal to the interests of the college," remarked a fellow professor, "and at no time, when called upon did he refuse to give service, though not officially bound to do so."

Four years later, Young was put in command of white soldiers at Camp Algers in Virginia. Many of the soldiers resented the presence of a black officer. One even refused to salute Lieutenant Young. The camp commander called Young and the soldier to his office. He asked Young to take off his coat and hang it on a chair, and he ordered the soldier to salute Young's jacket. Then the commander had Young put his coat back on, and he ordered the soldier to salute again. It was possible to salute the uniform, the commander explained, and not the man in it.

Young tolerated the army's insults, and in 1904 he attained the rank of captain. Accompanied by his new wife, Ada, he traveled to the Caribbean nation of Haiti, on the island of Hispaniola, as America's first black military attaché. Upon his arrival, a Haitian newspaper called Young "a handsome Black with distinguished bearing and charming manners." His knowledge of French, Haiti's official language, made him popular with the Haitians.

Young found himself in a small, mountainous, tropical country. At the turn of the century, the interior of Haiti remained largely unexplored and unmapped. Young traveled all over the island from the capital city of Port-au-Prince, where he was stationed. In some remote spots, he was the first foreigner the Haitians had ever seen.

The black officer drew up the first modern maps of Hispaniola and forwarded them to the United States War Department in Washington, D.C. The maps were to be of great help to the American military forces in 1915, when the United States occupied Haiti to restore order following political turmoil.

Young prepared detailed reports on many aspects of Haitian life, from agriculture to social customs to the magical rites of the West Indian religion called voodoo. He also compiled a dictionary of the widely spoken dialect Haitian Creole. In the introduction to his dictionary, Young explained that grunts and gestures were essential to Creole communication. He wrote that these noises and motions "are relic of the dark days when the Negro dared not express his feelings for the injustice and cruelty received from his master, and when a gesture or an 'oh' varied from a surprise to a prayer or mild protest. The Creole has not lost its charm and forcefulness in this regard after 100 years of freedom."

An energetic worker, Young wrote a play based on the life of François Dominique Toussaint L'Ouverture, who had led the struggle to liberate Haiti from French control and free the nation's slaves. While in Haiti, he also wrote a book, *Military Morale of Nations and Races,* a carefully researched study of the factors affecting soldiers' mental state and efficiency in battle. After studying the military histories of nations throughout the world, Young concluded that "there are no inferior races." To him, African Americans were in a position to bring about social changes that would benefit all Americans. He anticipated the civil rights movement of the 1950s and '60s when he wrote, "All progress and all advance in human society is made by the force and energy of minorities, who by their suggestion of policies and ideals, who by their leadership and often martyrdom, clear the obstacles to advance and give character to the masses."

Ada Young returned to the United States in 1906 to give birth to the couple's first child, Charles Noel. A daughter, Aurelia, was born three years later.

Charles Young saw another part of the world in 1912, when he accepted the job of military attaché in Liberia. When the famous black educator Booker T. Washington encouraged him to take the position, Young replied that he needed no persuasion. "I am always willing to aid in any work for the good of the country in general and our race in particular," he wrote, "whether the race be found in Africa or the United States."

Monrovia in the early 20th century was a rough, rustic place. Swamps bordered the city on three sides, and tropical diseases thrived. Young himself endured an attack of blackwater fever. Termites ate away at houses and government buildings; a Liberian official broke his leg when he fell through the weakened floor of the American Legation headquarters!

In spite of the hardship, Charles Young was soon his usual, busy self. He reorganized the Liberian army and started to explore inland regions. He traveled to many remote spots by boat or on foot. "Captain Young is at work preparing a map of the republic," reported the American ambassador soon after Young's arrival.

Liberia's tribes interested Charles Young as much as its geography. He reported on the Bassa, who were farmers, and the Vai, who wove fine cloth and had a well-developed sense of beauty. The Kru people, Young wrote, were "enterprising, hard-headed, sea-faring men. . . ."

On August 28, 1912, three months before leaving to rescue Captain Browne, Young was promoted to the rank of major. And in February 1916, he was back in the United States, standing before a crowd of 3,000 in Boston to receive the Spingarn Medal for his work in Liberia. The National Association for the Advancement of Colored People awards this medal to African Americans for outstanding achievement.

It was a proud moment for Major Charles Young, but he was always happiest when there was work to be done. He had been following the news from Europe, and it seemed to him that America was headed toward war. England and France had been fighting against Germany and Austria-Hungary since 1914. Officially, the United States was a neutral nation. But after a German submarine torpedoed a British ocean liner, the *Lusitania,* killing numerous innocent passengers, many Americans sided against Germany.

Young set up a training camp to prepare African Americans to command troops in the event of war. And his concerns soon

Boys of Liberia's Kru tribe in the early 20th century.
(Library of Congress)

proved correct. German aggression grew more intense, and on April 16, 1917, Congress declared war on Germany. The United States entered World War I.

Charles Young was now a colonel and the highest-ranking African American in the army. He was an accomplished officer and a capable leader who wanted some responsibility in the war. Army commanders, though, were not about to give Young the authority he had earned. Although 367,000 black enlisted men and officers would take part in World War I, Colonel Young would not be among them.

On July 7, 1917, Young received orders to have a physical examination. Army doctors found him to have high blood pressure and the beginnings of kidney trouble—and to be unfit for service in the war. Young's superiors offered him the command of a black company in the United States, but, discouraged, he retired from the army instead. He was 54 years old and had been a loyal officer for 29 years.

The doctors' pronouncement weighed on his mind, however, and in June 1918 he decided to prove his fitness for service in the war. He mounted a horse in Wilberforce, Ohio, and set off for Washington, D.C. Traveling by horseback and on foot, he completed the 500-mile trip in 16 days.

The colonel's feat impressed the army's commanders so much that they recalled him to active duty. But they sent him back to Liberia, and not to war. Young's new assignment caused an outcry from African Americans. If he were fit enough to take on a rigorous assignment in Africa, people asked, why couldn't he fight in Europe? The army never provided a satisfactory answer.

Still, Young was as industrious as ever, and more willing than before to speak up about the injustice he saw. He reported to the U.S. government that the Americo-Liberians were mistreating the native people. He wrote frankly about the beating of chiefs, the imprisonment of tribesmen for forced labor, and, most troubling of all, the practice of keeping tribal children as slaves. The native people were receiving nothing from their government but "slavery and oppression under the guise of trying to do them good," he wrote.

Not until 10 years later, in 1931, would investigators from the League of Nations confirm that Young's reports were accurate. Slavery would be abolished in Liberia in 1936.

On his second trip to Africa, Young journeyed to Nigeria, approximately 800 miles east of Liberia. He was collecting information for a book about Africa that he planned to write. In Lagos, the capital of Nigeria, his kidney ailment worsened. Colonel Charles Young died on January 8, 1922.

In 1923, the army returned Young's body to the United States for burial in Arlington National Cemetery, across the Potomac River from Washington, D.C. The black schools in the segregated city of Washington closed on the day of Young's funeral, and many children attended the service with their parents. Speaking to the gathered mourners, Army Chaplain O. J. W.

Scott praised Young's ability to make the best of unfair situations. The chaplain said, "Colonel Young believed a man laughs a thousand times where he weeps but one."

Chronology

March 12, 1864	Charles Young is born in Mays Lick, Kentucky
1882	teaches grammar school in Ripley, Ohio
1884	enters the United States Military Academy at West Point
1889	graduates from the academy as a second lieutenant in the U.S. Army; begins service on the frontier
1894	teaches military history at Wilberforce University
1904	marries Ada Mills; travels to Haiti as military attaché
1904–1907	explores the geography and culture of Hispaniola, drawing maps and writing reports
1912–1915	as military attaché in Liberia, makes exploratory trips to the nation's interior; earns the praise of President D. E. Howard for rescuing Liberian troops
1916	receives the Spingarn Medal for outstanding achievement in Liberia
1917	Young is denied a command in Europe during World War I; retires from the army
1918	rides from Ohio to Washington, D.C. on horseback to prove his fitness; returns to active duty and is assigned once more to Liberia
1921	reports to the U.S. government on the mistreatment of Liberian natives
1922	Charles Young dies in Lagos, Nigeria
1923	Young is buried at Arlington National Cemetery

Further Reading

Altman, Susan. *Extraordinary Black Americans from Colonial to Contemporary Times.* 1989. Chicago: Children's Press. Includes a short chapter on Young.

Chew, Abraham. *A Biography of Colonel Charles Young.* 1923. Washington, D.C.: R. L. Pendleton. A tribute to Young published shortly after his interment at Arlington National Cemetery.

Greene, Robert Ewell. *Black Defenders of America: 1775–1973.* 1974. Chicago: Johnson Publishing Company. Provides an account of Young's life and career, with quotes from historic documents.

———. *Colonel Charles Young: Soldier and Diplomat.* 1985. Washington, D.C.: R. E. Greene. A carefully researched report on Young's military career.

———. *The Early Life of Colonel Charles Young: 1864–1889.* 1973. Washington, D.C.: Department of History, Howard University. Chronicles Young's life from birth through graduation from West Point.

Heinl, Nancy G. "Col. Charles Young: Pointman." *Army,* March 1977. A biographical summary that takes a fresh look at Young's health records.

Wakin, Edward. *Black Fighting Men in U.S. History.* 1971. New York: Lothrop, Lee and Shepard. Features an account of the army's treatment of Young at the time of World War I.

Young, Charles. *Military Morale of Nations and Races.* 1912. Kansas City, Mo.: Franklin Hudson Publishing Company. Young's book about the psychology and battlefield behavior of soldiers.

Matthew Henson
(1866–1955)

Matthew Henson.
(Library of Congress)

---

*I*n 1990, scientists in Southern California took off in helicopters and headed for the North Pole, the northernmost point on Earth. They planned to study the polar ice cap from the air, to learn whether it could support future military operations.

In January 1994, the *Wall Street Journal* reported that the North Pole has become a popular tourist destination. Vacationers celebrate at the pole with champagne and barbecues, the *Journal* stated.

With research stations, military bases, and oil and gas pipelines, the polar region seems far less remote than it did a century ago. Then, the frigid Arctic was a place of mystery. No one had been to the North Pole. The public admired the explorers who braved the Arctic's subzero temperatures, intense winds, and vast expanses of ice. Those explorers risked their lives to bring honor to themselves and to their nations. They gained knowledge that would enrich the entire human race.

Since the time of Henry Hudson's explorations, in the early 17th century, daring individuals had ventured into the unknown northern realm. Some went looking for a "Northwest Passage," a northern trade route from Europe to the East. Others hoped to set a record for "farthest north," the highest northern latitude to be reached by human beings.

Some northern explorers met with disaster. An English team led by Sir John Franklin set out in 1845 and disappeared in the Arctic. Seven years later, Dr. Elisha Kent Kane, an American, went north, he said, "to conduct an expedition in the Arctic Seas in search of Sir John Franklin." Kane had another purpose as well: to reach the North Pole. Kane never found the pole, but historians believe he was the first explorer to travel with the Inuit, the people native to the Arctic who are sometimes called Eskimos.

A British party set a record for farthest north in 1876 at 83° 20′ north latitude. (The North Pole is at 90° north latitude.) Conditions were so arduous that 12 of the 15 explorers died. A survivor insisted that even if a group had the best equipment, "the latitude attained by the party I had the honour and pleasure of commanding, would not be exceeded by many miles."

Yet six years later, a team led by Lieutenant Adolphus Greely of the United States Army beat the British record by 6.9 miles. Theirs was a harrowing ordeal. People read in horror how Greely's party became stranded, ran out of food, and ate their shoes and clothing. They even consumed their dead. Only seven of the 25-member team survived.

In 1909, two Americans made history when they reached the North Pole. One of those men was Robert E. Peary of the United

States Navy. The other was Matthew Henson, an African American.

━━━━━━━━━━━━

Matthew Alexander Henson had few memories of Charles County, Maryland, where he was born on August 8, 1866. When he was a young child, his parents moved with him to Washington, D.C. Matthew's parents, who had been members of the free black population before the Civil War, cheered the ending of slavery in 1865, and saw it as a new beginning for their race. They came to the nation's capital seeking opportunity.

But the elder Hensons died before they could realize their dreams. At eight, Matthew went to live with his uncle. He attended the N Street School in Washington, where he learned to read and work with numbers. He studied maps during his geography lessons, maps that showed a world of exotic nations and vast oceans and continents.

Matt attended school through the sixth grade, and then he took off on his own. According to some accounts, he ran away to escape beatings at home. Matt made his way to the busy port of Baltimore, Maryland, 30 miles away. He signed on as a cabin boy on the *Katie Hines,* a ship bound for the Far East.

The *Katie Hines* took Matthew through the Strait of Magellan, the channel that separates the southern tip of South America and the island of Tierra del Fuego, and connects the Atlantic and Pacific oceans. During the five years that Henson spent aboard the *Katie Hines,* the ship docked in Japan, China, the Philippines, France, Spain, and North Africa.

As cabin boy, Matt served meals to the ship's commander, Captain Childs, and cleaned the captain's cabin. He washed dishes and assisted the cook. He also received a broad education. The ship's carpenter taught him to build sea chests and bunks. From the ship's mechanic, he learned to repair machinery. His favorite teacher, however, was Captain Childs.

The captain saw that his cabin boy learned quickly. He taught Matthew how to navigate, or direct a ship's course on the ocean. He encouraged the boy to read. Childs counseled Matthew on standing up to racial prejudice. "Your fight is with the ignorance in people's minds," Childs told the boy, "and your best weapons are knowledge and intelligence. These books are the beginning. Make them your fists, Matthew."

In 1883, when the *Katie Hines* was headed back to its home port, Captain Childs died. Matthew was devastated. He felt as if he had been orphaned all over again. He left the ship when it reached Baltimore, resolving to work on land.

The teenaged Matthew Henson had acquired useful knowledge and skills, but he could find no job that let him use his abilities. He became a messenger, a night watchman, and a servant. He labored on the Baltimore waterfront, loading cargo onto ships. Discouraged, Henson returned to Washington, D.C., where he worked as a stock boy at a men's clothing store.

One day in 1887, a man came to the store to buy a sun helmet to protect his head in the tropics. He was Lieutenant Robert E. Peary, 31 years old, a civil engineer with the United States Navy. Peary was on his way to Nicaragua, to choose a site for a canal. The government wanted to construct a waterway connecting the Atlantic and Pacific oceans in Central America. With such a canal, ships traveling east and west would no longer have to sail all the way around South America, as the *Katie Hines* had done.

Peary needed a servant, and he asked Henson to come along on the trip. Henson agreed to go; although he was qualified to be much more than a servant, he hated to pass up a chance to visit another part of the world. And in Nicaragua, he proved his worth to Peary. The lieutenant soon had Henson managing his entire camp of 45 engineers and 100 Jamaican laborers.

The United States never built a canal in Nicaragua. The government chose to put one in Panama instead. That decision was a great disappointment for Peary, an ambitious man who had hoped that working on the canal would earn his place in history. So Peary now focused on a new goal. He confided to Henson that, one day, he would cross the vast ice cap that covers central Greenland. He suspected that Greenland might provide an overland route to the North Pole.

Henson returned to his job at the clothing store while Peary raised money for the Greenland trip. Then, in September 1889, the world learned that a Norwegian, Fridtjof Nansen, had crossed the southern portion of the Greenland ice cap. Not to be outdone, Peary announced that he would cross the ice cap in northern Greenland, a trip that would be longer and more difficult. Peary asked Matthew Henson, who had been so helpful in Central America, to accompany him to Greenland; Henson immediately accepted.

In June 1891, Peary, Henson, and their team set sail in a small ship, the *Kite*. A voyage to the Arctic had to be timed carefully, since a ship could plow through the icy northern waters to dock in Greenland only in summer. Once there, the group had to set up a camp where they would wait out the winter, when the sun shines little or not at all. Henson would spend many winters in the Arctic, but he would never get used to the darkness, the silence, and the cold of that long, bleak season.

The explorers hired Inuit men and women to hunt their food and fashion their clothing from animal skins. Henson befriended the Inuit, and they taught him how to survive in the Arctic. They showed him how to hunt walruses and caribou, build an igloo, and construct and drive a dog sled. Arctic travelers transported all of their food and supplies on heavy sleds, or sledges.

"I have been to all intents an Esquimo," Henson later wrote, "with Esquimos for companions, speaking their language, dressing in the same kinds of clothes, living in the same kinds of dens, eating the same food, enjoying their pleasures, and frequently sharing their griefs." The Inuit felt a kinship with Henson, because his dark skin resembled their own. They called him *Miy Paluk*, meaning "Matthew the Kind One."

Spring brought lengthening periods of daylight, allowing the explorers to set out across the ice. The journey had to be made quickly. With the coming of summer's warmth, the ice would grow dangerously weak.

His eyelashes and mustache white with frost, Henson returns from a hunt with an Inuit campanion.
(Dartmouth College Library)

The explorers soon found themselves in a region of "glorious bleakness," Henson said, of "beautiful blackness." Most of the team turned back because of the cold. A frozen heel forced Henson to turn around. The Inuit refused to travel on the ice cap at all, believing it to be the home of an evil spirit. Peary and a single companion, the Norwegian Eivind Astrup, completed the 1,200-mile crossing of the ice cap. Peary discovered a large inlet, which he named Independence Bay. A land route to the pole, however, eluded him.

Their mission accomplished, the explorers arrived in New York in September 1892 to public acclaim. Peary and Henson toured the nation, showing curious audiences examples of their sleds, dogs, tents, and clothing. Henson demonstrated sled driving.

Peary and Henson made several more trips to Greenland in the years that followed. They embarked for the second time in

June 1893, and, as before, set up winter quarters. Their party was a large one this time, consisting of 12 men, Peary's pregnant wife, and a nurse. The following spring, when Peary set out to cross the ice cap once more, he surprised Henson by failing to invite him along. Only someone with a college education would be able to handle any possible emergencies, Peary explained.

Peary and seven other men left on March 6. They returned to the winter quarters after traveling just 128 miles onto the ice cap, illness and frostbite having forced them to turn back. Most of the white, college-educated team members decided Arctic life was too hard and returned to the United States in August. Mrs. Peary, her baby, and the nurse went with them. Peary, Henson, and a third man, Hugh Lee, stayed in Greenland. Peary had no choice but to have Henson accompany him in the spring of 1895, when he next ventured onto the ice.

Henson had learned his lessons in survival well, and he was invaluable in the frozen wilderness. He constructed igloos and handled the sledges as skillfully as an experienced Inuit. Alongside Peary, he fought off starving dogs that had turned on their human companions. After crossing the ice cap, he returned to the winter camp near starvation himself, but knowing he had made the expedition a success. Matthew Henson had become the first African American to cross Greenland's ice cap. Never again would Peary question his ability to handle an emergency.

The Americans saw many wonders in Greenland, including three large meteorites lodged in the earth. They hoisted two of the meteorites—weighing 1,000 pounds and 5,500 pounds—onto their ship for the voyage home.

Henson was sure that this trip to the Arctic had been his last. He had had enough of the cold and the hardships. "When I left for home and God's country," he wrote, "it was with the strongest resolution to never again! no more! forever! leave my happy home in warmer lands."

But he went back to Greenland with Peary over the next two summers, to retrieve the largest meteorite. Removing the third meteorite was a real feat of engineering: It weighed between

70 and 100 tons, and had to be moved to the ship from a spot 80 feet above sea level and 300 yards away!

The meteorites were put on display at the American Museum of Natural History in New York City, along with artifacts the explorers brought back from the north. The museum's officials were so impressed with Matthew Henson's knowledge of the Arctic that they hired him to prepare educational exhibits.

Peary by now had determined that Greenland was an island. He would never find a land route to the pole. Anyone going to the North Pole, he understood, would have to travel over the frozen Arctic Ocean. He asked Henson to go with him and give it a try, warning that the trip could last four years or more. Henson resigned from his job at the museum, and in 1898 he, Peary, and Dr. T. S. Dedrick, a physician, arrived in the Arctic. They were ready to take on their greatest challenge.

These three men and their Inuit companions set up a winter camp on Ellesmere Island, across a channel from northwest Greenland. But Peary was restless. A Norwegian group camped 43 miles away was planning a dash to the pole as well. Peary decided in December 1898 to move his party to Adolphus Greely's abandoned quarters, 250 miles to the north.

Arctic travel is most dangerous in the dark, frigid winter. Temperatures plunge below -60° Fahrenheit. Storms pack winds strong enough to move boulders. Snow that felt to Henson like "granules of sugar" stings the faces of travelers.

Peary's feet froze during the journey to Greely's camp. When Henson helped him remove his boots, most of the lieutenant's toes fell away. Dr. Dedrick persuaded Peary to return to the ship for surgery on his feet. The team made a second hazardous winter journey, returning with their injured leader on one of the sledges.

Peary's feet healed quickly, but he had to learn to walk on the ice and snow all over again without his toes. The men remained in Greenland, and it was not until April 6, 1902 that Henson, Peary, and four Inuit men started their sprint for the pole. Trekking over the unstable ice of the frozen ocean was more difficult than anything they had ever tried to do. In some spots, pressure had forced the ice into ridges 60 feet high. The explorers cut paths over the ridges with their axes. They then labored alongside their dogs, pulling the sledges up the slopes.

Ocean water flowed beneath the frozen surface. Its currents caused the ice to move constantly. The men took frequent compass readings to avoid drifting miles off course. There was always a danger, too, that the ice would split open beneath a person, or that he would be standing on a patch that suddenly broke away and floated off to sea. "A false step by any one would mean the end," Henson stated.

At times the group encountered leads, or expanses of moving water that blocked their advancement. The largest one they came upon, called the Big Lead, was more than a mile wide. Waiting for a lead to freeze used up valuable time. Floating across on a drifting piece of ice saved time, but was risky.

Progress was painfully slow. After 16 days of travel, the team had covered 82 miles, averaging 5.1 miles a day. Peary was ready to give up. As he wearily planted an American flag in the ice to mark the northernmost point reached by the expedition, he said, "I cannot accomplish the impossible."

That August, when they docked in the United States, Peary and Henson learned that reaching the pole might not be impossible after all. Italian explorers had set a new record for farthest north at 86° 34′ north latitude. The Italians had been 137 miles closer to the pole than the Americans. For Peary and Henson, there was no option but to try again.

"Only man can get a vision and an inspiration that will lift him above the level of himself and set him forth against all opposition," Henson said, "to do and to dare and to accomplish wonderful and great things for the world and for humanity."

Peary raised money for another expedition while Henson worked as a Pullman porter on the Pennsylvania Railroad. One evening, a friend in New York City introduced Henson to a bank clerk named Lucy Ross. The two fell in love and decided to marry after Matthew returned from one more Arctic trip.

That trip began in the summer of 1905. The *Roosevelt*, a ship named for President Theodore Roosevelt and designed to break through ice, carried Peary, Henson, and a new crew to the edge of the Arctic Ocean. The crew looked up to Henson as the Arctic expert aboard ship. He taught them the survival skills he had acquired so many years earlier.

Peary once had thought it unwise to allow Matthew Henson to explore the ice at his side. Now, he had so much respect for the African American that he asked Henson to lead the group toward the pole. "I can't get along without him," Peary said of his assistant. Henson pioneered a trail over unknown ice that the other sledge-drivers followed.

Henson led the others to a point 175 miles from the pole. The group set a new record for farthest north, 87° 6′ north latitude. But their food was running out, so they had to turn back.

President Roosevelt awarded Peary a gold medal for his achievement upon the group's return to the United States. Peary, however, still wanted to go farther. He still wanted to reach the North Pole. With Henson at his side, he would try once more.

Henson married Lucy Ross in September 1907. The following year, he sailed again for the north, "this time to be the last," he said, "and this time to win."

The *Roosevelt* reached Cape Sheridan, at the northern tip of Ellesmere Island, on September 5, 1908. On March 1, 1909, the team of explorers—white men, Inuits, and one African American—embarked "on what might be a returnless journey" to the pole, Henson said. The men planned to follow a straight line at 70° 27′ west latitude to the top of Earth.

Day after day, they battled ice and endured strong, relentless winds. "Our breath was frozen to our hoods of fur and our cheeks and noses frozen," Henson said. The group built igloos to shelter themselves at the end of each day's march. They ate meals of tea, biscuits, meat, and pemmican, a mixture of fat and dried meat. Henson repaired the sledges. As planned, some of the men turned back at intervals. This practice conserved supplies and lowered the risks to men and dogs. Nevertheless, one of those who turned back fell into the ocean and drowned.

THE ROUTE TO THE NORTH POLE, MARCH - APRIL, 1909

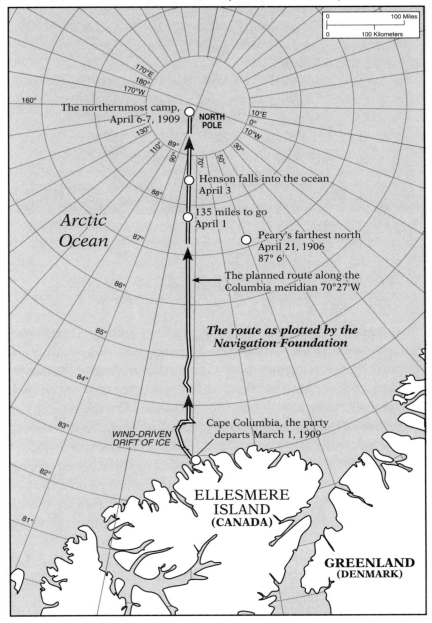

The Navigation Foundation used Peary's data to plot the route he and Henson took to the North Pole. The men planned to follow the Columbus meridian: shifting polar ice took them slightly off course.

Men, dogs, and sledges push toward the North Pole in March 1909.
(Dartmouth College Library)

By April 1, there were just 135 miles to go. Six explorers would complete the trip: Peary, Henson, and four Inuit companions. Henson almost did not make it. On April 3, he drove his sled onto a patch of thin ice. The ice gave out, and he fell into the black, numbing water of the Arctic Ocean.

Matthew Henson would have died without the fast action of Ootah, an Inuit team member. Ootah grabbed the hood of Henson's fur jacket and pulled him out of the water. Safe on land, Henson changed his boots, pounded the water out of his fur clothing, and continued the journey. In the Arctic, facing death and saving another's life were simply part of a day's work.

Three days later, Peary took a series of measurements that confirmed his hopes of success. He announced to Henson, "We will plant the stars and stripes—*at the North Pole!*" Henson brought out the American flag, and Peary took his picture holding it in the air, surrounded by the four Inuit at the top of the world.

And then, strangely, Peary's attitude toward Henson changed. He declined to shake hands with his longtime friend. He said little to Henson as they returned to the *Roosevelt,* and treated him like a servant aboard ship. Was Peary unwilling to share the credit for reaching the pole with a black man? The reason for his behavior is unclear. When Peary was later asked by Navy officials why he had taken Henson and not a white companion to the pole, he belittled Henson's ability. Henson would have been unable to get back to the ship without a white man's help, Peary said.

The Navy accepted Peary's response. At that time, many white Americans doubted the intelligence of African Americans. They also thought blacks had a biological makeup suited to life in warm climates. The fact that Henson survived in the Arctic surprised many people.

Donald MacMillan, one of the white members of the expedition, came to Henson's defense. "Henson, the colored man, went to the Pole with Peary because he was a better man than any of his white assistants," MacMillan said.

Henson poses aboard ship with, left to right, team members Donald MacMillan and George Barup and Peary on one of the sledges used to cross the frozen Arctic Ocean.
(Library of Congress)

Scientists appointed by the National Geographic Society reviewed the records Peary kept during his trip and declared him the discoverer of the pole. The society honored Peary and one of his white assistants with gold medals. They ignored Matthew Henson. Captain Robert Bartlett of the *Roosevelt* concluded, "It is very evident that there is one reason only why Henson has not been honored—he is black." African-American organizations, such as the Colored Commercial Association, were alone in commending Henson for his achievement.

Although the relationship between Henson and Peary would never again be close, Henson asked the white explorer to write a foreword to his autobiography, *A Black Explorer at the North Pole*, published in 1912. Peary praised Henson in the foreword, as he had in earlier years. Henson's accomplishments proved that "race, or color, or bringing-up, or environment, count nothing against a determined heart, if it is backed and aided by intelligence," Peary wrote, Henson paid a visit to Peary in 1920, when the older man was dying.

Matthew Henson lived out his life quietly. He worked for a time as a parking garage attendant in Brooklyn, New York. Then he took a job at the Customs House in New York City, and stayed there until he retired at age 70. Henson lived to see his contributions acknowledged. He received a medal from the United States Congress in 1945, and enjoyed other honors as well.

Henson's long life ended in 1955, and he was buried in the Bronx, New York. In 1988, his body was moved to Arlington National Cemetery and reburied next to Robert Peary. His headstone reads, "Matthew Alexander Henson, Co-Discoverer of the North Pole."

Whether Henson and Peary actually stood at the pole has been disputed in recent years. Some critics have said that Peary's calculations were sloppy, or even faked. In 1989, the Navigation Foundation, experts in determing position on the earth, reviewed Peary's data and photographs. The foundation concluded that if Peary and Henson did not actually reach the pole, they at least came very close. The issue may never be resolved

Chronology

August 8, 1866	Matthew A. Henson is born in Charles County, Maryland
1887	meets Lieutenant Robert E. Peary of the U.S. Navy; accompanies Peary to Nicaragua
1891–1892	Henson's first expedition to Greenland with Peary
1893–1895	the second Greenland expedition; Henson becomes the first African American to cross Greenland's ice cap
1896–1897	makes two trips to Greenland to retrieve a large meteorite
1902	first ventures onto the polar ice cap with Peary in an attempt to reach the North Pole
1906	leads an expeditionary force to a point 175 miles from the North Pole; sets a record for farthest north at 87° 6´ north latitude
1907	marries Lucy Ross
1909	Henson stands at the North Pole
1912	publishes his autobiography, *A Black Explorer at the North Pole*
1945	honored by Congress with a silver medal for "outstanding service to the Government of the United States"
1955	Henson dies
1988	Henson is reburied with honors at Arlington National Cemetery

Further Reading

Davies, Thomas D. "New Evidence Places Peary at the Pole." *National Geographic,* January 1990, pp. 44–61. A review of Peary's data by the Navigation Foundation.

Dolan, Edward F., Jr. *Matthew Henson: Black Explorer.* 1979. New York: Dodd, Mead & Co. A biography for young adults.

Ferris, Jeri. *Arctic Explorer: The Story of Matthew Henson.* 1989. Minneapolis: Carolrhoda Books, Inc. A biography of Henson for older children and teenagers.

Harrison, Paul Carter. *Black Light: The African-American Hero.* 1993. New York: Thunder's Mouth Press. Contains a brief section on Henson in a chapter on explorers.

Haskins, Jim. *One More River to Cross: The Stories of Twelve Black Americans.* 1992. New York: Scholastic, Inc. Includes a chapter on Henson's life.

Henson, Matthew A. *A Black Explorer at the North Pole.* 1989. Lincoln, Neb.: University of Nebraska Press. Henson's autobiography, first published in 1912, focuses on his 1908–1909 polar expedition.

Herbert, Wally. *The Noose of Laurels.* 1989. New York: Atheneum. Reviews the events and records of the Peary expeditions.

Albert José Jones

Albert José Jones.
(Albert José Jones, Ph.D.)

*I*t took three and a half hours for the boat, the *Island Diver,* to reach New Ground Reef, 35 miles southwest of Key West, Florida. On the deck, 12 people in black wet suits adjusted the tanks on their backs and fitted masks over their eyes. The twelve were experienced underwater adventurers, members of the National Association of Black Scuba Divers. It was May

1993, and the divers had come to this isolated spot on the Gulf of Mexico to forge a bond with history.

Thirty feet below, on the gulf floor, lay the wreckage of the *Henrietta Marie,* a slave ship that had sunk nearly 300 years earlier. The divers had come to place a plaque at the site, to remember the millions of Africans who had made the torturous, often fatal, journey toward slavery.

Albert José Jones, Ph.D. was one of the first divers to enter the murky water. A marine biologist and college professor, Jones had made some 5,000 dives during his long career. His fascination with undersea life had taken him all over the world, the Australia, North Africa, Asia, Central America, the Caribbean, and the South Pacific. He had been the first human being to dive in many places, and he had mapped coral reefs and offshore terrain.

Now, Jones and his fellow divers were preparing for a new experience, a trip back in time. "We're literally diving into our past," he said. Amid the wreckage of the *Henrietta Marie,* the divers would feel close to their forebears who had come to the New World as slaves.

Jones and another diver, Ric Powell, guided the massive concrete block bearing the plaque to its resting place on the sand, and the others followed. The concrete would soon become part of the undersea environment, as coral took hold in its crevices and thrived. Just before the block touched bottom, Jones gave it a turn so that the plaque faced east, toward Africa.

Diving conditions were far from ideal. A strong current ran through the water, and visibility was so poor that Jones strained to see a companion three feet away. Yet the divers lingered, reading and rereading the words cast in bronze: "*Henrietta Marie:* In memory and recognition of the courage, pain and suffering of enslaved African people. 'Speak her name and gently touch the souls of our ancestors.'"

Albert José Jones's first encounter with water took place on dry land. As a boy, he lay stretched out on a bench in his kitchen, face down, with his head over a full basin. He moved deliberately, kicking his feet and stroking the air with his arms. In a rhythm that matched his strokes, he took a breath, plunged his face in the water, exhaled, and then raised his head to the side. In the kitchen of his Washington, D.C. home, he was teaching himself to swim.

The water intrigued José, as Jones was called, and so did the animals that lived in it. He made many trips to a nearby creek to catch tadpoles, fish, turtles, and other creatures. By age eight, he had assembled a small zoo in his garage.

Orphaned at a young age, José was raised by an aunt and uncle who encouraged him to do well in school. Without an education, they warned, he would have no special skills or knowledge to offer an employer. "You have to be good at *something*," they said.

Young José needed little prodding to succeed. He loved going to school, and from kindergarten through high school, he rarely missed a day. At that time, Washington was a segregated city, where black and white children went to separate schools. Yet José never felt deprived. Rather, he felt lucky to attend the all-black schools in his neighborhood, because of their excellent teachers. With many careers closed to black professionals, intelligent, well-educated African Americans often taught in schools. Several of the teachers at Dunbar High School, from which José graduated, had earned their doctorates.

Those teachers were powerful role models for José. They instilled in him a strong desire to teach. Today, he reminds young people that they cannot succeed in any field without teachers. Doctors, lawyers, and other professionals all needed teachers to get where they are.

But before he could get the training he needed to become a teacher himself, José Jones spent three years in the army. Between 1950 and 1953, the United States took part in the Korean War, which began when Communist forces from North Korea invaded democratic South Korea. The United States was part of a United Nations force that fought on the side of South Korea to repel the Communist invaders. The Korean War was the first American military engagement since President Harry S. Truman had ended segregation in the armed forces in 1948; Jones and the other Korean War soldiers fought in integrated units.

Jones earned several medals for his actions in battle, including the Purple Heart, awarded to those who are wounded in combat. However, the two army experiences that most influenced his life occurred off the battlefield.

One day, while stationed in Korea, he was standing in an army "chow line," holding a tray and waiting to pick up his meal. It was an uncomfortable moment—another soldier was pushing around a small Korean man. Then, without warning, the Korean turned, executed a few quick moves, and had the bully on the floor. Jones had just seen his first demonstration of the martial art tae kwon do. Practitioners of this Korean form of karate use kicks and arm movements to overcome an opponent.

Jones was duly impressed. As soon as he returned to the United States, he found a teacher and began mastering tae kwon do. He stayed with it over the years, and today is ranked a sixth-degree black belt, designating an extremely high level of expertise. Eager to pass on what he has learned, he teaches free classes in the martial arts to young people in the District of Columbia.

Jones finished his military service in California, where army instructors taught him to scuba dive. The word scuba stands for self-contained underwater breathing apparatus. Scuba divers, or skin divers, carry Aqua-Lungs—tanks of compressed air—fastened on their backs. Tubes bring the air to a mouthpiece that controls its pressure. The pressure of the air inside the divers' lungs must equal the pressure of the water on their bodies. Scuba divers wear watertight masks over their eyes so they can see clearly below the water's surface.

The first time José Jones strapped on diving gear and jumped into a clear California lake, he felt a thrilling sensation that was entirely new to him: weightlessness. "You can be at a hundred feet, and you won't sink and you won't rise," he said. "You can just literally hang there." Like an astronaut in the weightless environment of space, he used his arms and legs to propel himself up and down, forward and backward. Jones had entered the quiet world of the animals he had studied as a child. And he had found another activity he would continue for life.

His army service completed, Jones enrolled in the District of Columbia Teachers College. It was "the best school I've ever been to," he said. Unlike many university professors, who stand in front of a class and lecture, leaving it up to the students to learn what they can, the faculty at D.C. Teachers College knew how to teach, Jones has said. They presented information and through discussion made sure the students understood it. Jones told himself that he would be that kind of teacher. He vowed to be able to teach well at all levels, to teach children and adults.

In 1959, Jones graduated from college with a degree in biology. That same year, he founded the Underwater Adventure Seekers (UAS), an organization for people interested in diving. Today, UAS is the oldest predominantly black scuba diving club in the world, and one of the oldest diving clubs in the United States. Its members have traveled the globe—from the Caribbean to the Red Sea, from Indonesia to the Fiji Islands—in search of new waters to explore.

Jones himself was off to Australia in 1960 to study on a Fulbright Scholarship. The U.S. government awards these financial grants to Americans wishing to study overseas, and the competition is keen. Jones spent nearly two years at the University of Queensland in Australia, observing underwater animals, such as the lionfish. This delicately beautiful fish requires careful handling, because its decorative spines are venomous. Jones made many dives in Australia's coastal waters to collect and photograph specimens of marine life.

José Jones continued his education in Washington, D.C. while he taught biology to junior high and high school students. In 1968, he earned a master's degree in aquatic biology from Howard University. Even after he took a job teaching marine biology at the newly formed University of the District of

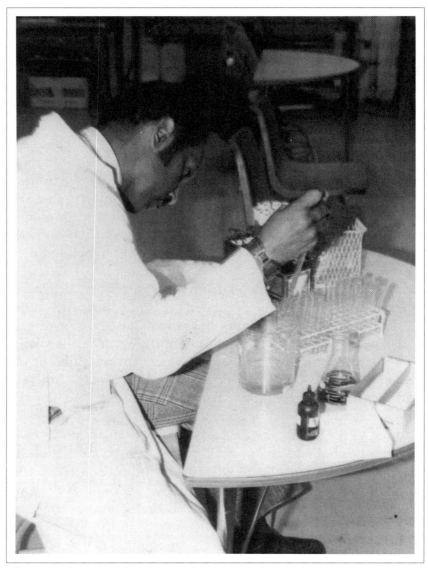

*A scientist as well as an explorer, Jones prepares biological specimens
for study.*
(Albert José Jones, Ph.D.)

Columbia in 1972, he followed his aunt and uncle's advice and kept on learning. In 1973, he fulfilled the requirements for a doctorate in marine biology from Georgetown University. He was named one of the Outstanding Educators of America in 1975.

At that time, Jones's research focused on marine animals and their behavior. He studied the reef fishes of the Caribbean, which include the sleek, sharp-toothed barracuda, the festively colored parrot fish, and the slithery garden eel. He turned his attention to sponges, those strange invertebrates that look more like leaves, tubes, and ropes than the animals that they are. But as he dove at different locations around the world, whether for research or for recreation, he noticed some alarming changes. Animals and plants seemed to be disappearing.

When the Underwater Adventure Seekers first visited the Caribbean island of Grand Cayman in the 1960s, they could simply walk into the water to find lobsters. As time passed, they had to venture farther and farther out to sea before they encountered a lobster. In the Caribbean and elsewhere, they saw fish populations declining and coral reefs shrinking.

Reefs are ridges of hard, calcium-containing material that take many years to grow on the sea floor. They are formed from the shells of tiny animals called polyps. Polyps thrive in colonies, with living animals building on the shells of their predecessors. Coral reefs form the basis of an ecosystem, where marine animals and plants live together in a fragile balance, depending on one another and their environment for survival. For example, algae and other plants grow on the reef's old skeletal surfaces, providing food for fish, sea urchins, sea cucumbers, and mollusks. Predatory animals such as crabs and sharks hide in the many crevices of a reef.

Change can occur quickly. In Indonesia in 1991, Jones swam through a pristine, untouched underwater landscape. He returned two years later to see a place that looked as if "dynamite had struck it," he said. "There were no fish, no coral. Fungus was growing all over the place."

Some of the damage Jones saw resulted from pollution. Household waste flowing into the water provides an abundance of nutrients for algae, which spread at an alarming rate, covering large sections of the reef and killing many polyps.

But pollution is not the only problem. Emerging countries, eager for tourism, harm the ecosystem when they build hotels and luxury homes on much of the available beach property. Bulldozers push silt into the sea, where it blankets the environment. In Indonesia and other tropical places, workers have uprooted the mangroves, the trees and shrubs that grow in shallow waters. Mangroves help to maintain the ecological balance in the brackish (slightly salty) waters where seas and rivers meet.

Certain fishing practices destroy the ecosystem as well. In some places, fishermen take too many fish—more than nature can readily replace. In other spots, dynamite really does strike. Fishermen explode dynamite in the water and collect the dead fish that float to the surface. Unfortunately, the dynamite kills all of the fish in the area of an explosion, not just the ones the fishermen want to harvest; many of the dead fish fall to the sea floor to rot.

Jones also acknowledged the troubling fact that "divers do a lot of damage." In the 50 years since Jacques Cousteau and Émile Gagnan developed the Aqua-Lung, millions of people have taken up scuba diving. The presence of so many humans stresses the reef environment. Anchors from divers' boats have struck and damaged many reefs. Divers often have taken chunks of coral as souvenirs. Jones asked, "If those of us who use this place don't take care of it, who's going to do it?"

Now Jones works with foreign nations to explore their coastal waters and recommend ways to preserve or repair the ecosystem. He starts by taking an "underwater census"—counting the fish, and the kinds of fish, in a region. This method can identify endangered species. He maps the underwater terrain, sometimes diving in places where no one has ever been. In 1989, he explored the entire coastline of Morocco,

For a marine scientist, the deck of a boat often serves as a laboratory.
(Albert José Jones, Ph.D.)

from the southern to the northern tip. In 1992, he surveyed marine life in the Red Sea, off the coast of Egypt.

Always a teacher, Jones brings his students along to help with research. The foreign beaches and waters become classrooms where Jones teaches reef ecology and research, chemistry, geology, and meteorology. The students learn about the people and culture of the country they are visiting, and they take on challenging projects. A group of Jones's students is surveying a reef in Belize, on the east coast of Central America, that will one day be part of a national park.

It can be difficult to persuade fishermen to stop employing harmful techniques. But if water conditions allow it, governments can import stocks of fish in an effort to raise the population. They can replant the mangroves, as Indonesia did, or regulate the construction of hotels, as Belize is doing.

Nations can help protect their coral reefs by placing buoys in the water at spots where divers frequently moor their boats. The divers can then anchor their craft on a buoy, and not on the reef below. And divers themselves must take care to protect the easily damaged ecosystems of their dive sites.

Albert José Jones is a private man who prefers not to discuss his personal life, including his date of birth. When it comes to sharing what he has learned, however, he is outgoing and enthusiastic. He has been teaching people to dive for more than 30 years. The Underwater Adventure Seekers have trained and certified more than 2,000 divers. And as with tae kwon do, Jones has never accepted a fee for teaching someone to dive. In 1991, he and some fellow divers started a new organization, the National Association of Black Scuba Divers (NABS), to bring together people with similar interests from across the United States and to encourage African Americans to take up diving.

Around that time, Jones and the other black divers learned about a discovery made in the Gulf of Mexico in 1972. Divers searching for one wrecked ship had stumbled upon another. They had found a slave ship, one of only three to be located in the Americas. An archaeologist named David Moore recovered artifacts from the ship over a 10-year period, bringing back pewter spoons and platters, cannons, muskets, and swords. He retrieved trade beads—colorful trinkets given to African traders who sold other blacks into slavery. The most distressing find of all was 80 pairs of rusted shackles and manacles once locked on the ankles and wrists of people imprisoned during voyages across the ocean. Some were small enough to fit young children.

Moore's discovery of the ship's bell bearing the name *Henrietta Marie* allowed historians to trace the vessel's route during its final voyage. Old records showed that the *Henrietta Marie* left London in 1699 to pick up 350 slaves on the west coast of Africa. People were stacked up inside the 60-foot ship, filling every possible space.

Jones and fellow diver Oswald Sykes stand with the plaque that now marks the site of the Henrietta Marie.
(Albert José Jones, Ph.D.)

The *Henrietta Marie* reached Jamaica and unloaded its human cargo in 1701. It is not known how many people survived the journey, but about one fourth of all Africans taken captive during the years of the slave trade died before reaching their destination. The ship's two captains received 19 English pounds for their load, about 40 dollars in today's currency. The crew then filled the ship with cotton, sugar, tobacco, and other goods and set sail for England. The *Henrietta Marie* sailed around the western side of Cuba and into the Gulf of Mexico, where it crossed paths with a heavy storm. The ship hit a reef, broke in two, and sank.

Hearing about the sunken ship and the tiny shackles convinced Jones of the need to honor the Africans taken into slavery. He and other NABS members spent 18 months obtaining the plaque and preparing to put it in place. Jones then started working to have an exhibit of *Henrietta Marie* artifacts travel to cities throughout the United States. In an interview for *Dive Trainer* magazine, Jones explained that the slave ship and its artifacts have importance for everyone, not just divers and not just African Americans. "People realize this isn't black history," he said, "this is American history. World history."

Today, Dr. Albert José Jones chairs the Department of Environmental Science at the University of the District of Columbia, where he has never missed a day of work. He and his students are assisting the government of Belize in its effort to develop tourism and protect its underwater resources. People often comment about Jones's many accomplishments. He always responds that there is no secret to success other than "to decide what you're going to do, then just do it."

Chronology

1959   Albert José Jones receives B.S. degree from the District of Columbia Teachers College; becomes a secondary school teacher; founds the Underwater Adventure Seekers (UAS)

1960   wins a Fulbright Scholarship to study at the University of Queensland in Australia

1968   earns M.S. degree from Howard University; first UAS dive at Grand Cayman

1972   joins the faculty of the University of the District of Columbia

1973   receives his Ph.D. from Georgetown University

1975   elected to Outstanding Educators of America

1989   surveys marine life along the coast of Morocco

1991   first dive in Indonesia; co-founds the National Association of Black Scuba Divers (NABS)

1992   inventories marine life in the Egyptian Red Sea

1993   Jones and other NABS divers lay a plaque at the site of the sunken slave ship *Henrietta Marie*

1995   works with the government of Belize to protect coastal marine life

Further Reading

Cottman, Michael. "Plunge Into a Painful Past." *New York Newsday,* May 27, 1993. An article on black divers' efforts to memorialize the *Henrietta Marie.*

Narine, Dalton. "Black Underwater Divers." *Ebony Man,* October 1989. A profile of Jones and the Underwater Adventure Seekers.

———. "Blacks Invade the Deep Blue Sea." *Ebony,* September 1988. Describes the popularity of scuba diving among African Americans.

Schultz, Adele R. C. "Keeping up With Jones, UDC's Renaissance Man." *Washington Post,* January 10, 1980. A biographical sketch of Jones and his many interests.

Stiefel, Vicki. "Dr. Albert José Jones: Sharing the Message of Success." *Dive Training,* June 1994. Outlines Jones's activities as a diver and as a mentor for youth.

Sullivan, George. *Slave Ship: The Story of the Henrietta Marie.* 1994. New York: Cobblehill Books. An account for young readers.

University of the District of Columbia Alumni Journal. March/April 1995 edition. A televised interview with Jones.

Weintraub, Boris. "Slave Ship Relics Inspire a Memorial." *National Geographic,* February 1995. Quotes Jones on the placing of the plaque at the site of the *Henrietta Marie.*

Author's note: Much of the information in this chapter was obtained during an interview with Albert José Jones. Dr. Jones was generous with his time, and I thank him.

Guion S. Bluford Jr.
(born 1942)

Guion S. Bluford Jr.
(NASA)

*I*t was 3:40 A.M., September 5, 1983. Powerful floodlights shone as bright as day on the Mojave Desert of California, where hundreds of people had gathered. They had come to watch the space shuttle *Challenger* descend through the dark sky and land on the brightly lit runway.

Like all of the shuttles, *Challenger* was part aircraft and part space ship. It had wings and landing gear like an airplane, yet it could leave Earth's atmosphere and travel in space.

Scientists at the National Aeronautics and Space Administration (NASA) had big plans for the reusable space shuttles. The shuttles could launch communications satellites or craft bound for distant space. One day, they might carry workers and supplies needed to build orbiting laboratories or space stations. They might ferry people between those structures and Earth. Right now, the shuttles served as laboratories themselves, allowing astronauts to carry out experiments in the weightless environment of space.

Challenger landed smoothly, coming to rest within 300 feet of its target. The crowd cheered the shuttle crew as they left their spacecraft. The applause was loudest for Lieutenant Colonel Guion S. Bluford Jr. of the United States Air Force, the first African-American astronaut. As a mission specialist, Bluford had been responsible for technical and scientific aspects of the flight. While in space, he had launched a satellite and performed delicate experiments.

Bluford spoke to the crowd. "I'm really humbled to see so many people out here," he said. "I feel very proud to be a member of this team, and I think we have a tremendous future with the space shuttle—I mean *all* of us."

A lifelong fascination with flight, combined with a desire to work hard and achieve, had brought Bluford to this historic moment.

Guy Bluford was born in Philadelphia, Pennsylvania on November 22, 1942. His father, Guion Stewart Bluford Sr., was a mechanical engineer. His mother, Lolita Bluford, was a teacher. Guy was born into a family of achievers. His relatives included several talented musicians, a college president, and a newspaper editor. Guy and his younger brothers, Eugene and Kenneth, learned early in life to do their best and strive for success.

A quiet, thoughtful child, Guy liked to solve crossword puzzles and play brain-teaser games. His favorite hobby was building model airplanes. As he glued the miniature planes together, he thought about the dynamics of flight—how the shape of an airplane's wing helps it lift into the air, for example, or how an aircraft creates a shock wave when it passes the speed of sound.

Guion S. Bluford Jr.

Guy never missed a chance to watch the way an object flew. Playing table tennis, he noticed how the angle at which he hit a ball affected its direction. Delivering newspapers in his integrated neighborhood, he tried folding the papers in different ways and then watching their flight as he tossed them onto doorsteps. He decided that when he grew up, he would be an aerospace engineer, someone who designs craft to travel in the atmosphere and beyond. No one had flown in space when Guy Bluford was a child, but some scientists were saying that the era of space travel would soon arrive.

Guy had a quick mind, but he seemed to learn better on his own than in the strict setting of school, where he had to work hard to keep up with his classmates. Still, he enjoyed tackling tough math and science problems. "He would sit very quietly until I began asking really hard and challenging questions," recalled one of Guy's high school science teachers. "Then he would come alive."

When Guy was nearly 15, the Soviet Union launched *Sputnik*, a 180-pound satellite, into orbit. The continuous beeping of *Sputnik*'s radio transmitters signaled to the world that exploration had entered a new domain. During their long history, humans had probed nearly every part of their planet. They had sailed to unknown continents, penetrated jungles, trekked to the poles, and investigated the oceans. Now, they had the technology to venture beyond Earth's atmosphere, into space.

President Dwight D. Eisenhower created NASA in 1958 to develop and implement an American space exploration program. Eisenhower directed that a group of space explorers—known as astronauts—be chosen from among the nation's military test pilots.

While the first astronauts were training for space flight, Guy Bluford graduated from high school and entered Pennsylvania State University to study aerospace engineering. He worked hard at his courses in science, mathematics, and engineering. And he paid attention to news about the latest achievements in space exploration.

In April 1961, Yuri Gagarin became the first person to travel in space when he rode in the Soviet orbiter *Vostok I.* Astronaut Alan Shepard made the first American manned space flight a month later. Shepard's tiny space capsule reached the upper limit of the atmosphere and then fell into the ocean 380 miles from its launch site at Cape Canaveral, Florida. Another astronaut, John Glenn, orbited the Earth in 1962.

American society was making forward strides as well. In the 1950s and '60s, African Americans made important gains in their quest for civil rights. For example, for 13 months starting in December 1955, the black citizens of Montgomery, Alabama boycotted their city's buses, demanding the same treatment as white riders. Their protest led to a ruling in federal court, allowed to stand by the Supreme Court, that segregated transportation violated the Constitution. In Birmingham, Selma, and other Southern cities, African Americans staged marches and sit-ins to assert their rights as citizens.

School kept Guy Bluford too busy to take part in civil rights demonstrations. Not only was he attending classes, but he had enrolled in the Reserve Officers Training Corps (ROTC) as well. The ROTC trains college students to be military officers. Bluford hoped to become an Air Force pilot after graduation. Knowing how to fly planes, he reasoned, would make him a better engineer.

While in college, Bluford started dating a fellow student, Linda Tull. The romance grew serious, and Guy and Linda married while still in school.

By the spring of 1964, Guy had a college degree in aerospace engineering and an officer's rank in the United States Air Force. Second Lieutenant Guion S. Bluford Jr. traveled to Williams Air Force Base in Arizona, where he trained to be a pilot.

America's military involvement in Vietnam was just beginning when Bluford earned his pilot wings, in January 1966. The Air Force sent him to South Vietnam as a member of the 557th Tactical Fighter Squadron. There, he flew 144 combat missions in an F-4C Phantom jet and earned 16 medals for bravery.

Guion S. Bluford Jr.

Guy Bluford returned to the United States in 1967, to rejoin Linda and their two sons, Guion III and James. At Sheppard Air Force Base in Texas, he taught new pilots to fly fighter jets. Bluford never lost his interest in the science of flight, though. He still wanted to be an aerospace engineer. He applied for admission to the Air Force Institute of Technology, located at Wright-Patterson Air Force Base in Ohio. He was accepted as a student in 1972, and received further training in aerospace engineering.

During the 1960s, NASA had launched numerous manned and unmanned space probes. The American space program reached a high point on July 20, 1969, when astronauts Neil Armstrong and Edwin "Buzz" Aldrin set foot on the Moon.

Bluford earned a master's degree in 1974. Then he went to work at the flight dynamics laboratory at Wright-Patterson. He tested new aircraft and helped to design planes that could fly faster and higher than the ones that already existed. At last, Guy Bluford had fulfilled his childhood dream: He was working as an aerospace engineer.

At the same time, he continued to attend classes at the Air Force Institute of Technology. He earned a doctorate in aerospace engineering in 1978. As part of his studies, Bluford did research on delta wings, the triangular wings on some aircraft. He examined how air moves around delta wings on planes traveling faster than the speed of sound.

Bluford explored other career opportunities. With NASA, he thought, he could use his skills as an engineer and possibly fly in space. Most of the spacecraft NASA launched in the 1970s were unmanned. The Mariner program explored Venus and Mars. The Viking craft looked for signs of life on Mars, while the Pioneer program focused on the outer planets and distant regions of space. NASA had not given up on sending astronauts into space, however. Since 1972, the agency's scientists and engineers had been at work on a project called the Space Transportation System (STS). They were developing the shuttle.

Bluford applied for astronaut training, even though the chance that he would be accepted was slim. NASA received more than 8,000 applications from prospective astronauts to fill a class of 35. Yet Bluford was one of the lucky ones. His training group included two other African Americans, Colonel Frederick D. Gregory and Ronald E. McNair Ph.D., as well as Sally K. Ride, Ph.D., who would become the first American woman to travel in space.

From the start of the space program in the 1950s, all American astronauts had been white men. Captain Edward Dwight, an African-American Air Force officer, began training for space flight in 1962 after President John F. Kennedy, wishing to further the progress of civil rights, asked to have a black pilot included in the program. Dwight left NASA in 1966, saying that he had been pressured to quit because of his race. President Lyndon Johnson appointed another black pilot, Major Robert H. Lawrence Jr., to the program. Lawrence died in the crash of a fighter jet at Edwards Air Force Base in California, in 1967.

It seemed to Bluford in 1978 that the officials at the Johnson Space Center in Houston, Texas treated the black and white astronaut candidates equally. He enjoyed every minute of his training. "It gives me a chance to use all my skills and do something that is pretty exciting," he said. "The job is so fantastic, you don't need a hobby. The hobby is going to work."

The future astronauts studied a variety of scientific subjects, including geology, oceanography, and astronomy. They underwent water survival training, in case they ever had to eject from a spacecraft over the ocean in an emergency. They learned what it felt like to be in a zero-gravity environment. Bluford and the others practiced carrying out their flight duties in a mock-up of a space shuttle.

Bluford spent three months learning to operate the shuttle's mechanical arm, which is used to move payloads such as satellites out of the orbiter's cargo bay. After a year of training, he was qualified to be a mission specialist, one of the men and women who carry out scientific experiments on space-shuttle flights.

Guion S. Bluford Jr.

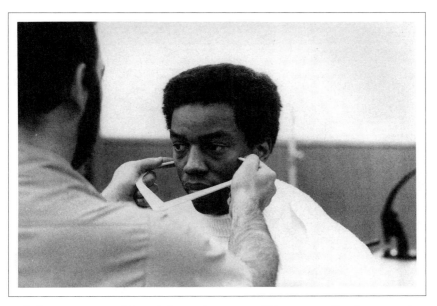

Bluford is measured for a helmet visor, part of his custom-fitted space suit.
(NASA)

At last, after years of research and testing, the STS was ready for flight. In April 1981, the space shuttle *Columbia* carried a crew of astronauts into space for the first time. Sally Ride made her historic flight two years later, aboard the shuttle *Challenger.*

When the eighth space shuttle mission was launched from Cape Canaveral on August 30, 1983, Guy Bluford was on board, about to become America's first black astronaut. The world's first black astronaut was Arnaldo Tamayo Mendez of Cuba, who flew in a Soviet spacecraft.

More than 200 prominent African Americans were on hand to watch the historic liftoff. The crowd included scientists, educators, and civil rights leaders. Actors Bill Cosby and Nichelle Nichols were there, and so was basketball star Wilt Chamberlain.

It takes a great deal of energy to propel a shuttle into space. An enormous external fuel tank powered the main engines

Bluford, suiting up.
(NASA)

aboard *Challenger* during the ascent. Two solid-rocket boosters provided extra lift.

As *Challenger* left Earth, flames lit up the sky. The air around the launch pad reached a temperature of 6,000° Fahrenheit. Within two minutes, the shuttle was 27 miles above the planet. The solid-rocket boosters fell away. Four minutes later, *Challenger* had reached the edge of the atmosphere. It was time for the main engines to shut down. The external fuel tank dropped off 180 miles above Earth, and *Challenger* went into orbit.

Space travelers enter an environment more hostile than any that has been explored on Earth. There is no air in space, and therefore no oxygen to breathe. There is almost a complete absence of heat in the shadows of planets, while temperatures in direct sunlight are high enough to kill. What's more, solar and cosmic radiation constantly bombard people and objects in space. On Earth, the atmosphere provides protection from this radiation. People can survive in space only if they are inside a sealed, temperature-controlled cabin or space suit. They need a steady supply of oxygen.

Bluford looked out of *Challenger*'s windows at his home planet far below. Traveling at 300 miles per minute and orbiting once every 90 minutes, he always saw a different view. Once, he gazed down at Florida, Cuba, and the Caribbean islands. On another orbit, he recognized the coastline of Louisiana. At times clouds covered the land masses, looking like enormous heads of cauliflower, or vast blankets of sheep's wool. At other times, sunlight reflected off the oceans as if they were glass.

It was a thrill to see the Earth in a way that few people had ever done, but the astronauts had jobs to do. Bluford and Mission Specialist Dale Gardner deployed, or launched, a weather satellite for the government of India. Once in orbit, this satellite would help Indian scientists predict floods and monsoons, the heavy winds that blow during India's rainy season. Advance warning of severe weather could help India save lives and property. The mission specialists ejected the satellite over the Pacific Ocean at sunset on the second day of their flight. "The deployment was on time," Bluford reported to Mission Control on Earth, "and the satellite looks good."

Bluford and Gardner carried out experiments on samples of body tissue in the weightless environment of space. They passed the tissue samples through an electrical field to separate the cells that produced hormones from the ones that did not. It was easier to do this in space than on Earth, because no gravity interfered with the process. Researchers hoped these tests would lead to a way to produce such substances as insulin, needed to manage diabetes, and anti-clotting agents, valuable in treating heart attacks, in orbiting laboratories.

The astronauts communicated regularly with the mission control staff on Earth. At one point, President Ronald Reagan spoke to the astronauts aboard *Challenger*. He had a special message for Guy Bluford, the first African-American astronaut. "You," Reagan said, "are paving the way for others, and you are making it plain that we are in an era of brotherhood here in our land."

Astronaut Bluford traveled aboard the *Challenger* again in the fall of 1985. On this mission, German and American scientists performed 76 experiments together. Bluford and the other scientists grew crystals and observed the behavior of fluids in space. They also released a satellite.

Guy Bluford continues to work and achieve. In the spring of 1991, he served on the crew of the space shuttle *Discovery*. He gathered environmental information on that trip and performed several experiments. In 1992, he was one of five astronauts who carried out military experiments in space for the Defense Department.

In July 1993, Bluford retired from the Air Force and NASA. He started a new career, directing engineering services at NYMA, a high-tech company. In spite of his many successes, Guy Bluford still finds it hard to believe that his longtime goals and hard work have carried him so far. As he explains, "I look at my life and I'm amazed that I've had the opportunities to do the things I've done."

Chronology

November 22, 1942	Guion S. Bluford Jr. born in Philadelphia
1958	President Eisenhower establishes NASA
1961	Yuri Gagarin orbits the Earth; Alan Shepard becomes the first American in space
1962	John Glenn orbits the Earth
1964	Bluford graduates from Pennsylvania State University with a degree in aerospace engineering; enters the Air Force
1966	earns his pilot wings; begins a tour of duty in Vietnam
1967	is assigned as an instructor pilot at Sheppard Air Force Base, Texas
1969	Neil Armstrong and Edwin Aldrin walk on the Moon
1974	Bluford is granted a master's degree from the Air Force Institute of Technology
1978	earns a doctorate in aerospace engineering; enters the astronaut training program
1981	the space shuttle *Columbia* orbits the Earth
1983	Guion Bluford becomes the first African American to fly in space, as a mission specialist on the space shuttle *Challenger*
1985	flies aboard *Challenger* for a second time

Black Explorers

1991	serves on the crew of the orbiter *Discovery*
1992	carries out military experiments on *Discovery*
1993	Bluford retires from the Air Force and NASA to work in private industry

Further Reading

Arnold, H. J. P., ed. *Man in Space: An Illustrated History of Spaceflight.* 1993. New York: Smithmark Publishers. Provides facts and many color photographs documenting the history of space flight.

Bigelow, Barbara Carlisle, ed. *Contemporary Black Biography, Volume Two.* 1992. Detroit: Gale Research. Includes a concise profile of Bluford.

Burns, Khephra, and William Mills. *Black Stars in Orbit.* 1995. San Diego: Harcourt, Brace and Company. The story of African-American involvement in space flight with background information on the black fighter pilots of World War II.

Haskins, Jim, and Kathleen Benson. *Space Challenger: The Story of Guion Bluford.* 1984. Minneapolis: Carolrhoda. A biography of Bluford for young readers.

Hawkins, Walter L. *African American Biographies: Profiles of 558 Current Men and Women.* 1992. Jefferson, N.C.: McFarland & Co. A brief account of Bluford's life and work.

Phelps, J. Alfred. *They Had a Dream: The Story of African-American Astronauts.* 1994. Novato, Calif.: Presidio Press. Contains a chapter on Bluford and an overview of black participation in the astronaut program.

Mae C. Jemison
(born 1956)

Mae C. Jemison.
(NASA)

*T*he space shuttle *Endeavour* was speeding over North America at 17,500 miles per hour, from the Pacific Ocean to the Atlantic. Mae Jemison M.D. may have been making history aboard the spacecraft, but she looked relaxed in her blue sweat pants. Thanks to a signal beamed down from space, her image appeared on two large television screens at the Museum of Science and Industry in Chicago, Illinois. It was the evening of

Mae C. Jemison

September 16, 1992. Students from all over the Chicago area waited their turn to speak into a microphone, to ask questions that would be broadcast via radio to the first African-American woman in space.

One young person wanted to know how long a day was on the shuttle. Jemison replied that it was short: Because *Endeavour* traveled so fast, the astronaut experienced only 48 minutes of daylight followed by 48 minutes of darkness. A middle-school student wondered how the astronauts mixed liquids in a gravity-free environment. It seemed to him that opening their containers would cause the liquids to escape uncontrollably. Jemison picked up a silver package and squirted a liquid into the air, showing how it shaped itself into bubbles that hung as if suspended.

When a seven-year-old asked if the astronauts had seen any other space ships, Jemison laughed. "I've been pretty busy working and haven't had too much time to look," she said. "I haven't seen any yet, but then again, I haven't looked everywhere yet."

A student from Morgan Park High School stepped up to the mike, and this time Jemison asked a question of her own. "Is Mr. Coleman still teaching science?" she inquired. "If he is, say 'hi' to him." The astronaut had graduated from Morgan Park in 1973. For her, the high-tech link with the Chicago students was a long-distance call home.

At last, the shuttle whizzed past the East Coast and the conference ended. Jemison and the rest of the crew returned to their experiments, gathering data that would aid future space travelers on longer, more distant missions.

Mae Jemison's curious mind had led her to explore a broad range of scientific and technical fields, from astronomy and chemistry to engineering and medicine. It had lured her to Africa and Asia and ignited her dream of flying in space. Now, she hopes she is just the first of many black female astronauts. "It is important that we start recognizing that every individual in society has skills and talents," she has said. She urges other Americans not to "be so closed that we picture scientists and explorers and adventurers as one kind of stereotyped person. We lose a lot as a society when we do that."

━━━━━━━━

Mae Carol Jemison was born in Decatur, Alabama on October 17, 1956. When she was three years old, her family moved to Chicago, the city founded by Jean-Baptiste Pointe du Sable, so the children could enjoy the many educational opportunities that city life offered.

Charlie Jemison, a maintenance supervisor, and Dorothy Jemison, a teacher, valued learning and achievement. They made many trips with Mae and her brother and sister, Charles and Ada, to the Museum of Science and Industry and to the Field Museum of Natural History. Early on, Mae developed diverse interests. She drew, climbed trees, and danced. Most of all, though, she liked learning about science.

When Mae started kindergarten, her teacher questioned her about what she wanted to be when she grew up. Mae responded that she planned to be a scientist. "Don't you mean a nurse?" the teacher asked. Like many people in 1960, the teacher believed that the world of science was a place for men. Young Mae refused to be swayed. "Now, there's nothing wrong with being a nurse, but that's not what I wanted to be," she said as an adult. She held on to her plan to study science, explaining, "I was stubborn."

Mae asked endless questions about plants and animals, rocks and minerals, and outer space. As soon as she knew how to read, she started checking out science books from the library. She read about the evolution of the Earth, about dinosaurs and other extinct creatures, and about the stars and planets. She even read many science fiction stories.

As a teenager, Mae excelled in her classes at Morgan Park High School. Her name was always on the honor roll. One day, she went on a field trip to a nearby university, where scientists showed her class how they performed experiments in their laboratories. They were doing work in biomedical engineering, which they predicted would be an important field in the decades to come.

Biomedical engineers develop artificial organs and limbs. They also use technology to diagnose and correct medical problems. The pacemaker, a device implanted in the chest to correct an irregular heart rhythm, is an example of a medical tool perfected by biomedical engineers. Students of biomedical engineering must master a variety of scientific fields, including chemistry, biology, and physics. Mae thought that she, too, would like to have a career that required knowledge of several scientific disciplines.

Mae Jemison graduated from high school in 1973, when she was 16 years old. That fall, she entered Stanford University, in California, on a National Achievement Scholarship. She worked hard in college and continued to pursue many interests, completing the requirements for degrees in chemical engineering and African and Afro-American studies. She took part in dance and theater productions.

A college friend named Sam Denard was going to work for NASA after graduation. Knowing of Mae's longtime interest in space, Denard told her that NASA was now accepting a broader range of applicants into its astronaut training program. Previously, only military pilots had trained for space travel. Now, NASA was looking for men and women with degrees in mathematics, engineering, or science to train as mission specialists. The mission specialists would not pilot spacecraft. Rather, they would perform experiments and technical duties on space flights. Sam Denard thought his friend would make a great astronaut. He urged her to join the program.

Jemison still dreamed about space flight, but for now she had other plans. After graduating from Stanford in 1977, she entered the medical school at Cornell University in New York. It was time to learn about another scientific field, medicine.

Medical school presented Jemison with opportunities she had not expected. In 1979, with a financial grant from the International Travelers Institute, she went to Kenya to conduct health studies. She wrote a report on public health in that

African nation, and she suggested ways to provide better health care to the people. Jemison enjoyed living in the predominantly black society of Kenya, a place where she never encountered racial prejudice. She hoped to see more of Africa one day.

In 1980, Jemison had a chance to visit Asia. She was one of a group of Cornell medical students who flew to Thailand to work in a refugee camp. Thousands of Cambodians had fled their war-torn nation and sought safety in Thailand. Jemison and the rest of the medical team treated the refugees for malnutrition, tuberculosis, dysentery, and other health problems.

The following year, Jemison graduated from medical school. She returned to California to complete her internship, a program of hands-on medical training, at a Los Angeles hospital. In July 1982, Mae Jemison M.D. started work as a general practitioner in Los Angeles. But in just a few months, she was back overseas again.

Jemison went to Sierra Leone and Liberia in West Africa as the area's Peace Corps medical officer. She was in charge of health care for the Peace Corps volunteers and United States embassy personnel who lived and worked in the region. Jemison put in long, busy days. She supervised medical workers and laboratories, and wrote manuals for self-care. She developed guidelines for public health and safety for the volunteers, and saw that they were followed. In cooperation with the National Institutes of Health and the Centers for Disease Control, she conducted research on a hepatitis B vaccine, rabies, and schistosomiasis, an illness caused by a waterborne parasite.

"I was doing work that affected people's lives and whether they lived or died," Jemison told a reporter for *Florida Today.* "I learned to trust myself and work with myself and develop the confidence that I'm able to take care of things on my own."

In the summer of 1985, Jemison returned to Los Angeles and the practice of medicine. She continually thought about ways to use her scientific knowledge and skills, and to keep on learning. She thought more and more about the space program. Both a woman, Sally Ride, and an African American,

Guion Bluford, had flown on shuttle missions; perhaps it was time for an African-American woman to train as an astronaut. Mae Jemison applied to NASA.

But before NASA officials had fully reviewed her qualifications, a tragedy occurred, and the future of the shuttle program was in doubt. On January 28, 1986, the space shuttle *Challenger* exploded 73 seconds after liftoff. All seven of its crewmembers, including Christa McAuliffe, a high school teacher from New Hampshire, and Ronald McNair, an African-American astronaut, lost their lives. NASA postponed the next fourteen shuttle missions indefinitely, until scientists learned the cause of the accident and found ways to prevent it from happening again.

Like people all over the world, Jemison mourned the death of the astronauts. However, she refused to let the disaster affect her dream of flying in space. After investigators traced the explosion to faulty "O-ring" seals in one of the solid-rocket boosters, NASA announced that shuttle flights would resume. Jemison reapplied to the program and was accepted in 1987. After a year of training, she qualified as a mission specialist.

Astronauts have work to do on the ground as well as in space. At the Kennedy Space Center at Cape Canaveral, Florida, Jemison helped to ready the space shuttles for launching. She made sure the payloads were in order, and she checked out the thermal protection system, the tiles on the outside of the shuttle that shield the craft from heat upon re-entering the atmosphere. She tested the shuttle's computer software to be sure that it was working properly.

At last it was Jemison's turn to venture into space. She was chosen to be a mission specialist on the 50th shuttle flight, a cooperative effort between the United States and Japan. This mission, a scientific one, was nicknamed "Spacelab J." A Japanese crewman would accompany the Americans into space and perform some experiments. For several months before the scheduled liftoff, Jemison traveled between the United States and Japan, preparing for the mission.

On September 12, 1992, Mae Jemison was aboard the space shuttle *Endeavour* as it left Earth. *Endeavour* was the newest

Jemison's survival training involved parachuting from a plane.
(NASA)

shuttle, built to replace *Challenger*. It was a thrilling moment for the first African-American woman astronaut, one she had dreamed about. She understood that people around the world felt pride in her achievement. "It was the realization of many, many dreams of many people," she said.

She had brought along items that represented some of the concerns that were most important to her, such as education and racial equality. She carried a flag from the Organization of African Unity and proclamations from the Chicago Public School System and the Du Sable Museum of African-American History in Chicago. A poster advertising the Alvin Ailey Dance Theater reflected her enthusiasm for dance.

Jemison was especially proud of a banner from the Mae C. Jemison Academy in Detroit, Michigan. This school teaches science and mathematics to children in preschool classes through the second grade. The children are the same age Jemison was when she first had to fight stereotypes to pursue her interest in science.

Endeavour swung into orbit 184 miles above the Earth and flew over Japan. The crew divided themselves into two groups, the Red Team and the Blue Team. The Japanese crewmember, Mamoru Mohri, was a member of the Red Team, which performed experiments for Japan.

The Blue Team, of which Jemison was a member, went to work while the Red Team slept. The Blue Team conducted experiments for the United States. They studied how the human body adjusts to the absence of gravity in space. In an experiment that Jemison designed, they examined the effect of space travel on bone cells. Astronauts tend to lose calcium from their bones during long periods of weightlessness. The team also experimented with ways to administer intravenous fluids

Simulating a rescue at sea.
(NASA)

Mae Jemison floats in zero gravity as the space shuttle Endeavour
orbits Earth.
(NASA)

in a weightless environment. Experiments such as this should enable people living on space stations in the future to receive needed medical treatments.

Jemison was in charge of an experiment that tested how weightlessness affected the fertilization of frogs' eggs and the development of the tadpoles that hatched from them. She fertilized some of the eggs in zero gravity and some in a centrifuge, a machine that created conditions similar to the gravitational pull of the Earth. Jemison proved that amphibian reproduction does not depend on gravity. "What we've seen is that the eggs were fertilized and the tadpoles looked pretty good," she reported. The experiment was exciting, Jemison added, because it answered "a question that we didn't have any information on before!"

In the SAREX experiment, the astronauts talked by radio to schoolchildren all over the world. Jemison conversed with children and teens in Chicago. As *Endeavour* flew over Japan, Mamoru Mohri conducted "space classrooms": He talked to Japanese students about the feeling of weightlessness and about his experiments aboard the space shuttle.

Endeavour landed after eight days in orbit, bringing the seven astronauts and more than 400 tadpoles back to Earth. Mae Jemison came home to awards and festivities. Americans were proud of their first black female astronaut, but none were prouder than the citizens of Chicago. Jemison's hometown held a six-day celebration in her honor, which coincided with her 36th birthday, October 17, 1992.

The astronaut spoke at a homecoming rally at Morgan Park High School. The students, teachers, and alumni cheered and applauded as she entered the auditorium. Jemison told the crowd about her own early experiences. She recalled the kindergarten teacher who discouraged her from studying science, and she warned the teenagers to be wary of people trying to talk them out of pursuing their dreams. "Sometimes people want to limit you because of their own limited imaginations," she said.

Jemison had learned that "you have to understand and believe in yourself and do what it is you know you are capable of in spite of what anyone else may tell you." She knows that her achievements have shattered stereotypes and may make it easier for other women and members of minority groups to succeed. "People don't see women—particularly Black women—in science and technology fields," she has said. "My participation in the space shuttle mission helps to say that all peoples of the world have astronomers, physicists and explorers."

Traveling in space was the fulfillment of a dream for Mae Jemison. Yet less than six months after her shuttle flight, she resigned from the astronaut program. "I leave with the honor of having been the first woman of color in space and with an appreciation of NASA—the organization that gave me the opportunity to make one of my dreams possible," she stated.

It was time for Jemison to move in new directions. In January 1993, she accepted a position teaching about space technology and its benefits for developing countries at Dartmouth College in New Hampshire. She is taking part in Alafiya, a project that will use satellite telecommunication to improve health care in West Africa. She also oversees The Earth We Share, a summer camp where children from countries throughout the world come together to study global issues, such as population and the environment.

Meanwhile, African Americans continue to explore our world and beyond. During a flight of the space shuttle *Discovery* in February 1995, astronaut Bernard A. Harris Jr., M.D. became the first black to walk in space. He was one of two astronauts testing a redesigned space suit in cold temperatures. NASA wanted to know if the suit would protect workers building future space stations.

Because the flight took place in February, which is Black History Month, Harris dedicated his space walk to the accomplishments of all African Americans, past and present, from Estéban and the other early slaves in the Americas to Guion Bluford and Mae Jemison. As he stepped from the shuttle into the blackness of space, Harris carried on that tradition of achievement. "Here I come!" he exclaimed. "The weather's nice out here. What a beautiful view."

Chronology

October 17, 1956	Mae Carol Jemison born in Decatur, Alabama
1973	graduates from Morris Park High School
1977	earns degrees in chemical engineering and African and Afro-American studies from Stanford University
1979	as a medical student, investigates public health issues in Kenya
1980	administers medical treatment to Cambodian refugees in Thailand
1981	graduates from Cornell University's medical school
1982	Dr. Mae Jemison works as a general practitioner in Los Angeles, California
1983	serves as a Peace Corps medical officer in West Africa
1985	returns to practice medicine in Los Angeles; applies for position with NASA
1986	the space shuttle *Challenger* explodes after liftoff; NASA postpones future shuttle missions
1987	Jemison is accepted for astronaut training after NASA resumes shuttle flights
1992	becomes the first African-American woman in space as a crewmember on the shuttle *Endeavour;* is honored by the citizens of Chicago
1993	resigns from NASA; teaches at Dartmouth College and participates in global education projects

Further Reading

"Dr. Mae Jemison Becomes First Black Woman in Space." *Jet*, September 14, 1992. A summary of Jemison's life and career published the week of her historic flight.

Harrison, Paul Carter. *Black Light: The African American Hero*. 1993. New York: Thunder's Mouth Press. A short summary of Jemison's career in a chapter on explorers.

Hawkins, Walter L. *African American Biographies: Profiles of 558 Current Men and Women*. 1992. Jefferson, N.C.: McFarlarn & Co. Contains a biographical sketch of Jemison.

Hine, Darlene Clark, ed. *Black Women in America: An Historical Encyclopedia*. 1993. Brooklyn, N.Y.: Carlson Publishing Inc. Summarizes Jemison's accomplishments.

La Blanc, Michael L., ed. *Contemporary Black Biography, Volume 1*. 1992. Detroit: Gale Research, Inc. Includes a short factual review of Jemison's life and accomplishments.

"Mae Jemison: Coming In From Outer Space." *Ebony*, December 1992. A profile of Jemison.

Phelps, J. Alfred. *They Had a Dream: The Story of African-American Astronauts*. 1994. Novato, Calif.: Presidio Press. A chapter on Jemison in a comprehensive history of African-American astronauts.

Smith, Jessie Carney, ed. *Notable Black Women*. 1992. Detroit: Gale Research, Inc. An informative sketch of Jemison's life and career.

————. *Epic Lives: One Hundred Black Women Who Made a Difference*. 1993. Detroit: Visible Ink Press. Contains a biographical entry on Jemison.

Index

Page numbers in *italics* indicate illustrations.

Index